CLEMENT VII
AND
HENRY VIII

By the same Author:

CLEMENT VII
AND
HENRY VIII

BY

PIERRE CRABITÈS

LONDON

GEORGE ROUTLEDGE & SONS, LTD.,

BROADWAY HOUSE, CARTER LANE, E.C.

1936

PRINTED IN GREAT BRITAIN BY
MACKAYS LIMITED, CHATHAM

Dedicated to
my esteemed friend
The Right Reverend Monsignor Thomas Vincent Shannon
of the Archdiocese of Chicago
who has, however, not seen
a line of my manuscript
or discussed its theme
with me

CONTENTS

PREFACE

I HAD originally intended entitling this book *Henry the Eighth's First Divorce* and adding the sub-title : *The Pope's Point of View.* I feared, however, that some of my readers might have assumed that I had some kind of ecclesiastical authority for thus claiming to speak in the name of the Holy See. As nobody has seen my manuscript and as I have outlined my thesis to nobody I have preferred to avoid any possibility of a misunderstanding by presenting my work under the name of *Clement VII and Henry VIII.*

I do so all the more readily because Pastor, in his authoritative *History of the Popes*, says that " Clement has had no biographer and almost all the historians of his time, with Guicciardini and Giovio at their head, pass severe judgments upon him."

I do not agree with their verdict or with that of Pastor, the scholarly Catholic who seems to have been influenced by them. He says that " Clement has been called the most unlucky of Popes." I am afraid that his subconscious mind has been influenced by that consideration.

I fear that he and Guicciardini and Giovio have had their perspective thrown out of line because great portions of Germany were lost to the Catholic

Church during Clement's reign and because the disaffection of Henry VIII took place at the same time.

I dissent from the opinion of the many Protestant writers who, with absolute good faith, have brought in strong indictments against Clement. I think that they have misread the facts available to them. I consider that even at this late date this misunderstood Pope is entitled to have his memory defended before the bar of posterity.

At least two major criticisms may be made of this work. In the first place it may be said that it is surcharged with what is called special pleading. In the second it may be pointed out that it is overloaded with quotation marks.

Both charges will be well founded. Before sentence is passed upon me I ask that it be borne in mind, in mitigation of the penalty that awaits me :

(1) that my book is admittedly one of advocacy. I am pleading a case. I am defending a Pope who was condemned by his contemporaries and who, for over four hundred years, has found few, if any, " so poor to do him reverence." Advocacy begets special pleading. My presentation has the faults of its virtues :

(2) that I am a Catholic. I am convinced that a defence based upon masked batteries is far less effective than one assured by adequate, though exposed artillery, supported by a mobile garrison which does not fear to advance beyond its ramparts. It is my belief that the best way to repel an assault

is to face the attacking army and to seek to capture the enemy's guns.

I do not consider that the criticisms of Guicciardini and Giovio and the strictures of Pastor constitute the " enemy's guns " which it behoves me to silence. I hold that I cannot make out my case unless I am able to bring to bear, in defence of Clement :—

(*a*) source material and

(*b*) proof adduced from the writings of Protestant authors.

The English-speaking world will refuse to listen to me if my evidence bears a Catholic imprint. It will even be sceptical about source material. My only hope of establishing my contention is to stress the Protestant aspect of my facts.

Were I to fall back upon footnotes the inference might be drawn that I had, in the ardour of my advocacy, misinterpreted my data. If I use quotation marks, and plenty of them, this imputation will fall to the ground. My reader will be able to judge for himself to what extent I have succeeded in my effort. But I cannot be said to have distorted my proof.

This volume has grown out of a suggestion made to me by my friend, Herbert H. Ryland, Esquire, of Windsor. It was in his hospitable home that I put the finishing touches to my *Beneš, Statesman of Central Europe*. He proposed that I should write a life of Sir Thomas More.

I found that the subject had been pre-empted,

My survey of the field whetted my appetite to know more of it. These pages are the outcome of the interest thus aroused. I am indebted to my host for the keenest of intellectual pleasures—the defence of a just cause.

PIERRE CRABITÈS

CLEMENT VII
AND
HENRY VIII

CHAPTER I

THE DEFENDER OF THE FAITH

HENRY VIII had been King of England for fourteen years when Clement VII became Pope. An accomplished scholar, linguist, musician and athlete, he held a warm place in the hearts of his countrymen, but the security of his tenure was not beyond question. His father, Henry VII, had ascended the throne by wading through a field of blood at the battle of Bosworth (August 22nd, 1485), and his reign had been frequently disturbed by a succession of Yorkist conspirators and pretenders, to say nothing of other menaces.

The lassitude of the people after the long drawn out wars of the Roses, Henry VII's rigorous rule, Henry VIII's personal popularity and the adroit statesmanship of his minister, Cardinal Wolsey, all tended to make the Pope feel that England's internal peace would not be disturbed as long as the King lived. Henry VIII, born in 1491, was still in the prime of life when Clement thus surveyed the field, but the Catholic Church never forgets what has passed, she thinks constantly of the present and she rivets her attention upon the future.

The wars of the Roses, the undercurrent of unrest

B   I

during the reign of Henry VII, the draconian measures that he had felt constrained to take to assure the succession of his son, all told the Pope that it behoved him to inquire into the future in the light of the lesson taught by this series of events. Clement knew that popularity is not only fleeting and ephemeral but fickle and inconstant. The fact that the populace applauded the King to-day was no guarantee that he would not be hissed to-morrow. This contingency was made all the more possible by the fact that Henry, scholar, linguist, musician and athlete though he was during the early years of his reign, allowed himself to be too much effaced by his ambitious minister.

In that epoch of personal rule it was a hazardous thing for a Sovereign to cede the limelight to a subject. The Pope feared that some day it might suit the soaring ambition of Wolsey to remove his influence from the House of Tudor and transfer it to a bold Contender. Clement thus kept his thoughts centred upon the Cardinal's machinations and upon the primary importance of a male heir being born to Henry, who would thus circumvent whatever devious designs Wolsey might have had in mind.

It must not be forgotten that Clement VII was not only an Italian but a Medici, and that as such he may have been tempted to think in terms of *combinazioni*. Wolsey had twice been a candidate for the Papal throne. Twice had he and the Pope crossed swords. At the first encounter the victory had gone to Adrian VI. At the second, Clement had won. These two tests of strength had made him perhaps too prone to attribute to Wolsey *combinazioni*, which were Italian and not English. But be this as it may, there is no doubt that the Pope viewed with grave concern the circumstance that Henry VIII had no male heir and that England's interests —which were likewise those of the Catholic Church —would not be safeguarded until Providence had vouchsafed this boon to the King.

Henry's Queen, Catherine of Aragon, born 15th December, 1485, was still a young woman when Clement VII ascended the Papal throne. She had borne sons to her consort, but unfortunately they had either died at birth or shortly afterwards. A daughter, Princess Mary, was the only issue of the marriage living at the time that the new Pope's grave responsibilities caused him to devote special attention to conditions in England.

It did not take Clement long to realize that as no Queen regnant had yet ruled in England, the possibility of a civil war in that country had to be envisaged, should no male heir be born to the King. Hopes were obviously centred round the Queen. Her youth encouraged the Pope to feel that her prayers and those of the Catholic Church would be answered. Continental Europe was divided between Islam, the Greek Schismatic Church, Lutheranism and concomitant sects ; Spain was honeycombed with " treason " ; France had not that virile Catholicism which prompts nations to die for their faith.   Italy, for strategic reasons, could not even be considered.   Clement's thoughts were constantly dominated by the necessity of England's domestic tranquillity remaining unimpaired.

The personal equation stressed the Pope's interest in the House of Tudor.   Henry VIII had given emphatic and dramatic evidence of his devotion to the See of Rome and to the tenets of the Catholic Church.   At a time when the current was running strongly against the Papacy he had not hesitated to throw down the gage of battle to Luther.   He had boldly championed not only the dogmas of Catholicism, but had gone on record as a militant protagonist of Papal Authority.

It is tempting to lay special emphasis upon this latter feature.   It does not figure prominently in the text of what Henry wrote but it brings his utterance into its proper perspective.   To explain what we mean it will be necessary to begin by citing two dates.   One of them is December 10th, 1520, that momentous day when Luther posted up a notice inviting the Wittenberg students to witness the burning of the Papal bull that had been launched against him.

That act breathed defiance.   It was meant to be —and it was—a frontal attack upon the authority of the Holy See.   The German populace may not have been able to grasp the niceties of the controversy which Luther had launched when he had nailed on the door of the Wittenberg Church his ninety-five theses so that the crowd could see and read them.

The German princes may not have been capable of following the subtleties of the dispute between Tetzel and Luther which centred around the question of Indulgences. But both the German peasants and the German nobles knew what the latter was not only saying but doing when he burnt that bull.

The second date to which we shall refer is August 25th, 1521. It was then that Henry issued his memorable reply to a theological broadside launched by Luther during the preceding year. The attack had been made in Latin. It bore the title *De Captivitate Babylonica*. We are not passing judgment upon the cogency of its reasoning or the accuracy of its facts when we say that it was incomprehensible to the average man or woman of the sixteenth century. The King's reply was also written in Latin. It was just as unintelligible to the rank and file as was the manifesto which it had sought to refute.

The only thing that the laity of those days understood—and the only thing that is now generally remembered of the incident—is that Luther and Henry crossed swords. Public opinion of that epoch looked upon Luther not as a theologian who was opposed to Indulgences but as a monk who defied the Papal Authority, and the King of England personified the defence of the challenged Papal Authority.

The principle of the primacy of the See of Rome had dominated the controversy between the

Churches of the East and West.   Greek theologians had, it is true, at an early date formulated twenty-three points against the Catholic doctrine.[1]   As time went on this number increased until it is said that there are now one hundred and sixty obstacles in the way of a union between the two creeds.   But at the Synod of Nymphee, held in 1234, when the Greek indictment contained about a hundred counts, the committee in charge of the Conclave had reduced the doctrinal issues to two.

It is not impossible that a formula could have been found, either then or at Lyons in 1237, or at Florence in 1438-1439, which would have satisfied both schools of thought, had it not been that the Greek hierarchy and the Greek nation resolutely refused to recognize the primacy of Rome.

They were obsessed with the idea that Constantine had transferred the seat of government from the banks of the Tiber to the shores of the Bosphorus. This conception of the significance of the foundation of Constantinople made it impossible for them to admit that the See of Rome was the equal, much less the superior, of that of Byzance.   The obstinacy with which they held to this point and the blindness of their fanaticism are exemplified by the encouragement which they constantly gave to the Turks to come and save them from the Pope.

If we analyse the difficulties with which the Spanish crown was confronted shortly after the

---

[1] *Dictionnaire Apologétique de la Foi Catholique*, Paris, Beauchesne & Cie, 1911, Vol. II, verbo Grecque (Eglise), p. 363 (*b*).

conquest of Granada we shall see that there, too, the issue, as the people of those days understood it, was not a question of heresy but of the defence of the prerogative of the State. In other words, in the East, in Central Europe and in the North, as well as in Spain or the West, it was the challenge to constituted authority, rather than doctrinal controversies which arrested universal attention.

We have stressed this point because it is pertinent to our theme. If the transcendent importance attached by the laity to the question of the assault upon Papal Authority made Henry VIII the outstanding champion of the Catholic Church, the ascendancy thus given him carried with it the corollary that the Papacy had a vital interest in adding to the lustre and security of his crown and of his dynasty.

It is a universal habit to think of issues in terms of men. The sixteenth century thus looked upon Henry as personifying the militant advocacy of Papal Authority. It is, therefore, obvious that the political strategy of the Church of Rome was directed towards maintaining the prestige of the Sovereign who incarnated the principle of her primacy. Anything that might have detracted from the renown of the English Monarch would inevitably have had its repercussion upon the advantage derived by the Papacy from having the whole world know that her prerogatives had the brain and the sword of Henry VIII at the back of them.

If the masses saw in the King's reply to Luther

evidence of an uncompromising advocacy of Papal Authority, Catholic theologians, while applauding this stand, were also delighted at the substance of his retort. It was expressed in a style that appealed to their hearts. It pulsated with the spirit of the age. It was so erudite and recondite that the initiated marvelled at its scholarship.

Luther had cynically refused to see in the sacraments of the Catholic Church anything other than " the devices of a human institution to hold its members by the most solemn ritual, taking them as they came in by baptism, holding them from month to month by penance and communion, catching them as they married by matrimony, nailing the priest by holy orders, ushering them out of the institution by extreme unction, and only needing for perfect discipline a sacrament of the tithes."[1]

To Henry's mind the Saviour had referred to the Catholic Church when He said : " Thou are Peter and upon this rock I will build My Church ; and the gates of Hades shall not prevail against it." He looked upon Luther as a fiend incarnate who was attempting to tear down an institution which the Lord had decreed should be eternal. He visualized his Church as his Mother and cried out : " I cannot but think myself obliged to defend my Mother, the Spouse of Christ." And, a scholastic of scholastics, he particularly resented his adversary's attack upon Saint Thomas Aquinas.

[1] *Henry VIII*, by Francis Hackett, London, Jonathan Cape, 1929, p. 185.

Henry's fighting blood, his devotion to his Church and his admiration of his own dialectical talents, urged him to take up Luther's challenge. " Our King," writes Lord Herbert of Cherbury in the quaint English of the seventeenth century, " (being at leisure now from warres, and for the rest delighting much in learning) thought he could not give better proof either of his zeale or education, then to write against *Luther*. To this also he was exasperated, that *Luther* had oftentimes spoken contemptuously of the learned *Thomas* of *Aquinæ*, who yet was so much in request with the King, and especially of the Cardinall, that (as *Polydore* hath it) he was therefore called Thomisticus. Our King hereupon compiles a booke, wherein he strenuously opposes *Luther* in the point of Indulgences, number of Sacraments the Papall Authority and other particulars."[1]

No sudden impulse prompted Henry to enter the intellectual lists against Luther. Even before the *de Captivitate Babylonica* was published " he had determined," as Brewer expresses it, " to signalize his theological acquirements and his devotion to the Church by writing against what he considered the prevailing heresies of the times."[2] We thus have the proof driven home that three important considerations lent zest to the King's reply to Luther.

[1] *The Life and Raigne of King Henry VIII*, written by the Right Honourable Edward Lord Herbert of Cherbury, London, Thomas Whittaker, 1649, p. 104.
[2] *The Reign of Henry VIII, from his Accession to the Death of Wolsey*, by J. S. Brewer, edited by James Gairdner, London, John Murray, 1884, Vol. I, p. 601.

They were : (1) long premeditation, (2) intellectual vanity and (3) devotion to the Church.

We shall not speak, for the moment, of the first two factors. We prefer to pass on to the third. We do so all the more readily because, in a letter to Pope Leo X, dated May 21st, 1521, Henry expresses his anxiety to suppress the Lutheran heresy and to write a book, " the first offspring of his intellect, that all men may see he is as ready to defend the Church with his pen as with his sword."[1]

The Pope was overjoyed at having such a stout champion who was " as ready to defend the Church with his pen as with his sword." When the thesis was presented to him, in solemn audience, by the King's Ambassador, assurance were given " that the Holy See would do as much for the confirmation of the King's book as ever was done for the works of St. Augustine or St. Jerome."[2] And, the next day, a Consistory was held and the title of *Fidei Defensor* or Defender of the Faith was conferred upon Henry, after those of *Protector*, *Defensor Romanæ Ecclesiæ* (Defender of the Roman Church), *Defensor Sedis Apostolicæ* (Defender of the Apostolic See), *Rex Apostolicus* (Apostolic King), *Rex Orthodoxus* (Orthodox King), had previously been privately debated among the Cardinals.[3]

The King's book was translated into German and published in Leipzig in 1523. An English version was also brought out and, " multiplied into many

---

[1] Brewer, *op. cit.*, Vol. I, p. 602.
[2] *Ibid.*, p. 605.
[3] Herbert, *op. cit.*, p. 104.

thousands by various printers, it filled the whole Christian world with joy and admiration." Everything thus tended to fix upon Henry the status of Rome's outstanding champion " who was as ready to defend the Church with his pen as with his sword."[1]

[1] Brewer, *op. cit.*, Vol. I, p. 606.

CHAPTER II

HENRY'S QUALMS OF CONSCIENCE

HENRY VIII was married to a princess five years his senior. The Queen, Catherine of Aragon, was a daughter of Ferdinand and Isabella of Spain. She was, wrote Ludovico Falieri, a contemporary Venetian Ambassador to England, " of low stature and rather stout ; very good and very religious ; speaks Spanish, French, Flemish and English ; more beloved by the Islanders than any queen that has ever reigned ; about forty-five years of age and has been in England about thirty years."

The world in those days knew nothing of willowy figures. Waistlines were then invariably neglected. No great importance need be attached to the diplomatist's reference to Catherine being of "low stature and rather stout." What brings out the fact that her beauty had faded is his statement that she was forty-five years old when we know that she was about thirty-nine when the world learnt that Henry's scruples had begun to plague him. When an Italian adds six years to the age of a Queen he means to say that she looks like an old woman.

The King, who was thus mated to a consort who

was five years his senior but who looked older than her age, is thus described by the same Ambassador :

" In the eighth Henry such beauty of mind and body is combined as to surprise and astonish. Grand stature, suited to his exalted position, showing the superiority of mind and character ; a face like an angel's, so fair it is ; his head bald like Cæsar's and he wears a beard, which is not like the English custom. He is accomplished in every manly exercise, sits his horse well, tilts with his lance, throws the quoit, shoots with his bow excellent well ; he is a fine tennis player, and he practices all these with the greatest industry. . . . He appears religious also generally hears two mass a day and, on holy days, High Mass besides."

Born at Alcala de Henares on December 15th, 1485, when her mother was moving about from place to place inspecting the armies of Castille, Catherine's infancy was passed amidst the storm of battle and siege. She accompanied her parents in their grand entry when Granada succumbed to the Christian forces. From that moment, until she left for England, the Alhambra was her home.

Destined to be a pawn upon the chessboard of international politics, Catherine was betrothed in 1497 to Arthur, the elder son of Henry VII of England and Elizabeth of York.

The young couple were allowed to correspond with one another for the double purpose of cultivating mutual affection and improving their Latin.

Arthur was her junior by about a year. He wrote her from Ludlow Castle in 1499 :

" I have read the sweet letters of Your Highness lately given to me from which I easily perceive your entire love to me. Truly these letters, traced by your own hand, have so delighted me and made me so cheerful and jocund, that I fancied I beheld Your Highness, and conversed with and embraced my dearest wife. I cannot tell you what an earnest desire I feel to see Your Highness and how vexatious to me is this procrastination about your coming."[1]

Two years were permitted to pass before, as an old manuscript puts it :

" Donna Catalina (Catherine) being at Granada with the King and Queen, there came ambassadors from the King of England to demand her for the prince of England, his son, called Arthur. The union was agreed upon, and she set off from Granada to England, parting from Alhambra on the 21st of May in the year 1501. . . . She embarked at Coruna 17 August. Contrary winds forced her vessel back on the coast of Old Castille which occasioned great illness to Donna Catalina. After she was convalescent, she embarked more prosperously on the 25th of September in the best ship they had, of 300 tons, and after a good voyage landed at a port called Salamonte (Plymouth) on the 2nd October, where the señora princess Catalina was grandly received with much feasting and rejoicing."[2]

---

[1] *Lives of the Queens of England*, by Agnes Strickland, Philadelphia, J. B. Lippincott Company, 1893, Vol. II, p. 472.
[2] Strickland, *op. cit.*, Vol. II, p. 472.

Arthur and Catherine met at East Hampstead a few days later. As they had previously been married by proxy, the King caused them to pledge their troth in person on November 14th, 1501. Bishop Burnet tells us in his *History of the Reformation of the Church of England* that :

" They lived together as man and wife till the 2nd of April following ; and not only had their bed solemnly blessed when they were put in it, on the night of their marriage, but also were seen publicly in bed for several days after, and went down to live at Ludlow Castle in Wales, where they still bedded together. But Prince Arthur, though a strong and healthful youth when he married her, yet died soon after, which some thought was hastened by his too early marriage. The Spanish Ambassador had, by his master's orders, taken proofs of the consummation of the marriage, and sent them into Spain ; the young Prince also himself had, by many expressions, given his servants cause to believe that his marriage was consummated the first night, which in a youth of sixteen years of age, that was vigorous and healthful, was not at all judged strange."[1]

It is but fair that we should add that Catherine, whom Bishop Burnet calls " a virtuous and grave Princess, much esteemed and beloved both of the King and the whole nation,"[2] and who was in a position to have first-hand knowledge of the fact of which the distinguished author thus writes with

---

[1] *History of the Reformation of the Church of England*, by Bishop Burnet, London, J. F. Dove, 1820, Vol. I, p. 54.
[2] Burnet, *op. cit.*, Vol. I, p. 56.

such dogmatic finality, fails to agree with him. We shall subsequently have occasion to hear her say to Henry : " And when ye had me at the first, I take God to be my judge, I was a true maid without touch of man ; and whether it be true or not, I put it to your conscience."[1]

We shall not attempt, at all events for the present, to pass upon the question of fact so categorically affirmed by Bishop Burnet and so unequivocally denied by Catherine with the more or less tacit approval of Henry. All that we shall say is that the death of Arthur played havoc with the plans of Henry VII and Ferdinand. They were misers and politicians who deplored the financial and strategic complications brought about by this unexpected demise. They consulted their own interests. They finally agreed that, on obtaining a dispensation from the Pope, Catherine should marry her young brother-in-law, Prince Henry.

Papal intervention was requested because it is written in the Scriptures that :

" Thou shalt not uncover the nakedness of thy brother's wife : it *is* thy brother's nakedness " and that

" Whosoever shall commit any of these abominations, even the souls that commit *them* shall be cut off from among their people."

Catherine seems to have been unhappy at this time. She wrote to her father " that she had no

---

[1] *Life of Cardinal Wolsey*, by George Cavendish, London, Thomas Davison, 1827, p. 215.

inclination for a second marriage in England, still she begged him not to consider her tastes or inconvenience, but, in all things, to act as suited him best."[1] Ferdinand took her at her word and on December 26th, 1503, a Bull was obtained from the Holy See and dispatched to England which read, in part :—

" That the Pope, according to the greatness of his authority, having received a petition from Prince Henry and the Princess Catherine, bearing,

" That whereas the Princess was lawfully married to Prince Arthur (which was perhaps consummated by the *carnalis copula*) who was dead without any issue, but they, being desirous to marry for preserving the peace between the crowns of England and Spain, did petition his Holiness for his dispensation.

" Therefore the Pope, out of his care to maintain peace among all Catholic Kings, did absolve them from all censures under which they might be, and dispensed with the impediment of their affinity, notwithstanding any apostolical constitutions or ordinances to the contrary, and gave them leave to marry."[2]

When this Papal Dispensation was received Henry was but twelve years of age. The marriage ceremony was performed shortly after its receipt,[3] but the young couple were kept apart. It was understood, however, that they were to live in wedlock as soon as Henry should attain the canonical age of

---

[1] Strickland, *op. cit.*, Vol. II, p. 487.
[2] Burnet, *op. cit.*, Vol. I, p. 55.
[3] *Ibid.*, p. 55.

C

puberty. But it appears that the Archbishop of Canterbury, Warham, had evinced such an aversion to this union that on the day the Prince became of age his father caused him to appear before Fox, Bishop of Winchester, and declare in the presence of a notary public that :

" Whereas he being under age was married to the Princess Catherine, yet now coming to be of age, he did not confirm that marriage, but retracted and annulled it, and would not proceed in it, but intended in full form of law to void it and break it off, which he declared he did freely and of his accord."[1]

Before the ink was dry upon this protest Henry VII hastened to assure Ferdinand of Spain that the Prince of Wales and Catherine would become man and wife at the first opportune moment and that this public renunciation was merely an idle formality. But he went to his grave on April 22nd, 1509, without having taken any steps to carry out this promise. Burnet assures us that, on the contrary, he charged his son to break off the union, not because religious scruples bothered him but because he feared " a controverted title to the crown."[2]

One of the first problems confronting the new Sovereign was that he must either definitely break off his marriage with Catherine or conclude it. Henry was heartily in favour of going on with the contract. The Privy Council debated the matter

[1] Burnet, *op. cit.*, Vol. I, p. 56.
[2] *Ibid.*, p. 56.

most earnestly. Warham, Archbishop of Canterbury, held to his view that the relationship in which Catherine stood to the King as his sister-in-law was too near. Fox, Bishop of Winchester, supported the expediency of the union. All the prelates and lawyers agreed that the protest filed by Henry on the eve of his attaining the canonical age of puberty gave him the legal right to refuse to carry out the agreement.

As so often happens when an important issue is joined, a compromise was arranged. It was agreed that the wedding should take place if Catherine's sister, Queen Joan, and their father, King Ferdinand, would agree that the marriage portion of the Princess should never be reclaimed on any pretence whatever. Fuensalida, the Spanish Ambassador, signed a deed to this effect on the part of Ferdinand as King of Aragon and of Joan as Queen of Castille. Catherine herself also affixed her signature to it.

A most regrettable mystery is made by some historians of the time and place of the marriage of Henry and Catherine. " Both," writes Agnes Strickland, " we have satisfactorily discovered in the pages of Catherine's native chroniclers. ' Donna Catalina,' says Bernaldes, ' wedded the brother of her first lord, who was called Enrico, in a place they call Granuche (Greenwich) on the day of St. Bernabo (June 11th, 1509) and was crowned afterwards, on the day of St. John, with all the rejoicing in the world.'

" Her father, King Ferdinand, was so well

pleased, adds another Spanish historian, at his daughter's second marriage that he celebrated it by grand festivals in Spain, particularly by the *jeu de cannes* or darting the jereed, in which Moorish sport Ferdinand assisted in person."[1]

It would seem as if these dispensations, protests, assurances and debates, followed by such rejoicing, could not fail to make an impression on Henry and direct his attention to the exceptional conditions surrounding his marriage. But his happiness appears, at first, to have been so unalloyed that he paid no attention to them. The years passed and it was only after he had seen his sons die, either at birth or shortly afterwards, that his ill-assimilated knowledge of theology began to plague him. His apologist, Herbert, thus tells us how his mind worked :

" Our King had now (1528) for many years enjoyed the Vertuous Queen Katherine, without either scruple of the validity of their Match, or outward note of unkindnesse had past betwixt them. Nevertheless, as presently after the Birth of the Princess (who alone of all their children survived) *Luther* and others controverted the authority and extent of the Papall Jurisdiction, so in this Kingdome, the Dispensation of *Julius* the Second for the aforesaid marriage, being privately questiond, many of our learned Men concluded it void and granted in a Case prohibited *Jure Divino*, and therefore indispensable.

[1] Strickland, *op. cit.*, Vol. II, p. 504.

" This again, whispered in the eares of many, begot such a muttering as being brought to the King made him think what Hee was to doe. For though Hee knew that the keeping of the Succession doubtfull was one of the ill arts by which princes conserve themselves ; yet, as a desire to have Posterity, which might succeed Him in the Crown, prevailed over all other Considerations, He resolved to clear this point by all fitting degrees."[1]

George Cavendish, Cardinal Wolsey's Secretary, supplements this statement by placing these words in Henry's mouth :

" And to put you all out of doubt, I will declare unto you the special cause that moved me hereunto (to inquire into the validity of the marriage with Catherine) ; it was a certain scrupulosity that pricked my conscience upon divers words that were spoken at a certain time by the Bishop of Bayonne, the French King's Ambassador, who had been here long upon the debating for the conclusion of a marriage to be concluded between the Princess, our daughter Mary, and the Duke of Orleans, the French King's second son."[2]

Burnet gives this version of the origin of the King's " scrupulosity of conscience " :

" On the first day of the year (1511) she (the Queen) made him a very acceptable new-year's gift of a son, but he died in the February thereafter : she miscarried often, and another son died soon after

---

[1] Herbert, *op. cit.*, p. 215.
[2] Cavendish, *op. cit.*, p. 219.

he was born ; only the Lady Mary lived to a perfect age. In this state was the King's family and the Queen left bearing more children, and contracted some diseases that made her person unacceptable to him. . . .

" The King being out of hopes of more children declared his daughter Princess of Wales, and sent her to Ludlow to hold Court there, and projected divers matches for her. The first was with the Dauphin, which was agreed to between the King of France and him the 9th of November, 1518, as appears by the treaty yet extant. But this was broken afterwards. . . .

" There was a second treaty begun with France, the King offering his daughter to Francis himself, which he, gladly accepting, a match was treated : and on the last of April (1527) it was agreed, that the Lady Mary should be given in marriage either to Francis himself or to his second son the Duke of Orleans. . . .

" But while this was in agitation the Bishop of Tarbes, the French Ambassador, made a great demur about the Princess Mary being illegitimate, as begotten in a marriage that was contracted against a divine precept, with which no human authority could dispense. How far this was secretly concerted between the French Court and ours, or between the Cardinal and the Ambassador is not known. It is surmised that the King or the Cardinal set on to the French to make this exception publicly, that so the King might have a better colour to justify his suit of divorce, since other princes were already questioning it."[1]

And having thus brought out the fact that the strictures which the Bishop of Tarbes placed upon Princess Mary's legitimacy were nothing but diplomatic camouflage suggested either by Henry or Wolsey, Burnet goes on to say :

" What were the King's secret motives and the true grounds of his aversion to the Queen, is only known to God : and till the discovery of all secrets at the day of judgment, must lie hid." This author then adds :

" But the reasons which he always owned, of which all human judicatories must only take notice, shall be now fully opened. He found by the law of Moses, if a man took his brother's wife they should die childless. This made him reflect on the death of his children, which he now looked upon as a curse from God for that unlawful marriage.

" Upon this he set himself to study the case and called for the judgment of the best divines and canonists. For his own inquiry, Thomas Aquinas, being the writer in whose works he took most pleasure, and to whose judgment he submitted most, did decide it clearly against him. For he both concluded, that the laws in Leviticus about the forbidden degrees of marriage were moral and eternal, such as obliged all Christians ; and that the Pope could only dispense with the laws of the Church but could not dispense with the laws of God ; upon this reason,

[1] Burnet, *op. cit.*, Vol. I, p. 57.

that no law can be dispensed with, by any authority, but that which is equal to the authority that enacted it."[1]

What Herbert and Cavendish and Burnet have told us is very interesting as far as it goes, but it does not carry us very far. It deals with the origin of that " certain scrupulosity that pricked " Henry's conscience, but it does not let us know when it began or when " Hee resolved to clear this point by all fitting degrees."

The only element that is available to us in seeking to find out when it was that conscientious scruples first began to plague Henry is furnished by his ungentlemanly want of delicacy in telling Simon Grynæus, a comparative stranger, who visited him in 1531, that he had abstained from the Queen's bed for seven years, that is to say from 1524.[2] He did not, however, then say anything about " those diseases that made her person unacceptable to him." We therefore have no way of knowing whether it was " scrupulosity of conscience " or fear of contamination that caused the robust man of thirty-three to take the decision which he so crudely announced to a man who was a mere acquaintance.

Confronted with such a condition a Frenchman would be tempted to apply his favourite maxim of *cherchez la femme*. This is what Audin does in his *Vie de Henri VIII*, which the Catholic Bishop of Digne assures us sets forth " the ferocity, sensuality

---

[1] Burnet, *op. cit.*, Vol. I, p. 59.
[2] Brewer, *op. cit.*, Vol. II, p. 162.

and astuteness " of that monarch with true fidelity to the facts of history.[1]   He unhesitatingly proclaims that it was the King's attachment for Anne Boleyn, one of Queen Catherine's ladies-in-waiting, that engendered the " certain scrupulosity that pricked " his conscience.   He wrestles with dates to make good his argument.

Opposed to this more or less plausible theory we have Froude's categorical assertion that :

" There was no trace at the outset (of the divorce case) of an attachment to another woman. . . . Anne Boleyn when it was first mooted was no more to the King than any other lady of the Court."[2]

It would seem an easy matter to examine the facts and see whether the Catholic authority or the Protestant historian adheres to the truth, but unfortunately we do not know when it was that Anne Boleyn first began to dominate Henry's thoughts. And while Burnet assures us that the King told Grynæus that he " had abstained from the Queen upon these scruples,"[3] such a statement does not preclude the possibility that he may have become an ascetic before 1524. It may be, as far as we know, that, at an earlier date, Catherine had " contracted some diseases that made her person unacceptable to him." We do not even know whether Anne Boleyn was comely or homely.

[1] *Histoire de Henri VIII*, by J. M. Audin, Paris, Maison, 1856, Vol. I, p. vii.
[2] *The Divorce of Catherine of Aragon*, by J. A. Froude, London, Longmans Green & Co., 1891, p. 25.
[3] Burnet, *op. cit.*, Vol. I, p. 59.

She is described by one author as :

" A little, lively, sparkling brunette, with fascinating eyes and long black hair, which, contrary to the sombre fashion of those days she wore coquettishly floating loosely down her back, interlaced with jewels. The beauty of her eyes and hair struck all beholders alike, grave ecclesiastics and spruce young sprigs of nobility . . . a beauty not so whitely as clear and fresh above all we may esteem, which appeared much more excellent by her favour passing sweet and cheerful."[1]

Another description of her takes this form :

" She was ill shaped and ugly, had six fingers, a gag tooth and a tumour under her chin, with many unseemly things in her person. At the fifteenth year of age both her father's butler and chaplain lay with her : afterwards she was sent to France where she was first kept privately in the house of a person of quality ; then she went to the French Court, where she led such a dissolute life, that she was called the English Hackney. Then the French King liked her, and from the freedoms he took with her she was called the King's Mule."[2]

We are convinced that there is not a word of truth in these attacks upon Anne Boleyn's early life. We have quoted such an outrageous libel merely to show that as we are dealing with a subject where partisanship knows no restraint we cannot be too careful about controlling the facts upon which we

[1] Brewer, *op. cit.*, Vol. II, p. 172.
[2] Burnet, Vol. I, p. 64.

rely. As we have no irrefutable evidence in regard to the time when Anne Boleyn entered the King's life or when his " scrupulosity of conscience " caused him to begin serious inquiry into the validity of his marriage, it strikes us that Burnet has properly summed up the case for us when he holds that " all human judicatories must only take notice " of " the reasons which he always owned."

CHAPTER III

THE COLLUSIVE SUIT

CATHERINE of Aragon was but thirty-nine years of age when Henry proclaimed that he had discovered that she had " contracted some diseases that made her person unacceptable to him." As long as she had remained beautiful and as long as the Spanish alliance had subsisted her position was unassailed. But when her eldest children died, people had already begun to predict that her marriage boded ill to the country. When she had lost the expectations and the attractiveness of youth, a crisis came in which England ceased to depend on the friendship of her family and was protected against their enmity by a close union with France.[1]

The motives that impelled Wolsey to take advantage of this strategic change are not shrouded in mystery. For a quarter of a century the strength of the Tudors had been the safety which their name inspired. When it became obvious that Catherine would have no son to inherit the crown, the old insecurity was revived. Men recalled what Civil War had carried in its wake and that during the seven preceding reigns murders had seven times determined the succession to the throne.

The Quarterly Review, No. 285, January, 1877, p. 7.

It may be assumed that Henry, who had been untrue to Catherine in earlier years, felt no impelling urge to be faithful to her when her beauty had waned. We may, therefore, take it for granted that Wolsey foresaw not only the possibility of a disputed succession but the reign of favourites who would make his position most insecure. He was far too great a patriot and far too ambitious a man to view with equanimity the perils that confronted England and the uncertainty that surrounded his own future.

To a prelate who thought in terms of higher politics rather than in those of religion, the reasons of state for dissolving the King's marriage were better than those which had recommended it to Henry VII. Trained in the subtle art of insinuation it was not a difficult thing for him to throw out cautious hints about the words of Leviticus and to innoculate the mind of the distressed Sovereign with the idea that the death of the three royal sons might perhaps be considered a penalty for transgressing God's will. It is not irrefutably proved that it was Wolsey who caused Henry to become obsessed with the idea that Heaven had put its curse upon him, but it is unmistakably established that this conception dominated the King's mind and caused him to appeal to the Church for relief.

Wolsey obviously had no thought of helping to release Henry from his marriage with Catherine in order to allow him to be fancy free. The Cardinal's mind was centred upon finding a bride who could give the King an heir, strengthen England's international position and also do away with the possibility of a reign of favourites. His thoughts naturally turned towards France. There he found two eligible princesses.

One of them, Renée, the Queen's sister, was ill-favoured and all but deformed. Henry was not likely to accept such a bride. The other was the King's sister, Margaret Duchesse of Alençon, a widow both talented and wealthy. But Francis had other plans for her and betrothed her to the King of Navarre on Christmas Day, 1526.

When Wolsey was thus considering the political aspects of Catherine's inability to provide the King with male issue, Herbert tells us that :

" Hee (Henry) took information sometimes about his present condition and (it is probable also) about such Ladyes as might furnish him a choice for a Geniall, and second bed. In which number the Dutchesse of *Alançon*, Sister to *Francis*, is the first I find mentioned, whose Picture (as Hall saith) was sent over, about this time."[1]

It would appear that the King, in taking information " sometimes about his present condition " and " about such Ladyes as might furnish him a choice for a Geniall, and second bed," became smitten with the charms of Anne Boleyn. Henry may have begun in 1524, for conscientious reasons, to absent himself from the Queen's couch, but what he learnt about

---

[1] Herbert, *op. cit.*, p. 216.

" his present condition," when Wolsey was scanning the capitals of Europe to find a suitable bride for him, convinced him that it was immaterial to him whether the Cardinal was or not successful in his search. He was not internationally minded like his Minister. Home talent appealed to him and the animal in him gained the ascendancy over the statesman.

Certain writers make it almost an article of faith to prove that the scruples of Henry preceded his proposal of marriage to Anne Boleyn. We have no evidence before us which would permit us to contradict their assertion. We are inclined to think that it is well founded. He had, somewhere about 1524, inoculated himself, or been inoculated by others, with the idea that his marriage with Catherine was of doubtful legality. He knew that the Cardinal was searching for a bride for him. A married man in such a frame of mind is most susceptible to the graces of a woman, even though she may be as immaculate as the driven snow.

The salient point which interests our narrative is that however innocent may have been the friendship between Anne and Henry during 1524, 1525 and 1526, " in 1527 it was buzzed about in every ear and every tongue was talking about it."[1] This is but another way of saying that when the King learnt, during the early days of 1527, that the Dutchesse of Alançon had been betrothed to the King of Navarre on Christmas Day, 1526, he was in a frame of mind

[1] Brewer, op. cit., Vol. II, p. 183.

that made it easy for anybody to catch him on the rebound.

Henry's pique at being disdained by Francis and the fact that he consoled himself for this chagrin by finding solace in Anne's smiles mean that during the early months of 1527 Catherine found an appointed rival. The "King's scrupulosity of conscience" then became pricked by something more urgent than his conception of religion. Passion, more than theology, began to dominate his mind. He pondered over the meaning of the texts of Holy Writ in the light of the joys he hoped to find in the arms of his favourite.

Wolsey soon heard of Henry's obsession. At first, he paid no attention to it. He assumed that the King, in courting Anne during his long absence from the Queen's boudoir, was taking " information sometimes about his present condition," and that she was facilitating him in setting his mind at ease. The idea did not dawn upon the Cardinal that Henry was thinking of the maid-of-honour in terms of matrimony. He took it for granted that she was but another Elizabeth Blount of fleeting fancy.

So completely did Wolsey misjudge the nature and extent of the King's passion that he unwittingly played a part in consolidating Anne's mastery over her royal suitor. It appears that

" Lord Percy, the son and heir of the Earl of Northumberland, then attended upon the Lord Cardinal, and was also his servitor ; and when it chanced the Lord Cardinal at any time to repair to the Court, the Lord Percy would then resort for his pastime into the Queen's chamber and there would fall in dalliance among the Queen's maidens, being at the last more conversant with Mistress Anne Boleyn than any other, so that there grew up such a secret love between them that, at length, they were insured together, intending to marry. The which thing came to the King's knowledge who was then much offended. Wherefore he could hide no longer his secret affection, but revealed his secret intendment unto my Lord Cardinal in that behalf ; and consulted with him to infringe the precontract between them."[1]

Wolsey, being a man utterly devoid of morality, judged the King by his own standards and assumed that Henry wanted to get rid of young Percy so that he could enjoy Anne as his exclusive preserve. No suspicion entered the Cardinal's mind that he was asked " to infringe the precontract between them " so that she might become Queen of England. He saw in the request made of him an opportunity to gratify his Sovereign's lust without impinging upon the domain of higher politics. We, therefore, learn that

" After my Lord Cardinal was departed from the Court, and returned home to his place at Westminster, not forgetting the King's request and counsel, being in his gallery called there before him the said Lord Percy unto his presence, and before us his servants of his chamber, saying thus unto him. ' I

[1] Cavendish, *op. cit.*, p. 120.

D

marvel not a little,' quoth he, ' of thy peevish folly, that thou wouldest tangle and censure thyself with a foolish girl yonder in the Court, I mean Anne Boleyn.   Dost thou not consider the estate that God hath called thee unto in this world ?   For after the death of thy noble father, thou art most like to inherit and possess one of the most worthiest earldoms of this realm. . . . Now behold what ye have done through your wilfulness.   Ye have not only offended your natural father, but also your most gracious sovereign lord, and matched yourself with one, such as neither the King, nor yet your father will be agreeable with the matter.' "

The upshot of this frontal attack by the Cardinal was that young Percy was forced to marry Lady Mary Talbot, daughter of the Earl of Shrewsbury

" by means whereof the former contract was clearly undone.   Wherewith Mistress Anne Boleyn was greatly offended, saying, that if it lay ever in her power, she would work the Cardinal as much displeasure ; as she did indeed after.   And yet was he nothing to blame, for he practiced nothing in that matter, but it was the King's only device.   And even as my Lord Percy was commanded to avoid her company, even so was she commanded to avoid the Court and sent home again to her father for a season ; whereat she smoked : for all this while she knew nothing of the King's intended purpose."[1]

It is quite probable that Henry himself did not then know how deeply he was in love with Anne or

[1] Cavendish, *op. cit.*, p. 129.

rather what a control his passion had gained over him. Had he realized the strength of his craving for her she would not have been " commanded to avoid the Court and sent home again to her father for a season." And she would not have smoked—or fumed—at the thought of the loss of her young flame, " for all this while she knew nothing of the King's intended purpose."

Looking back at the matter across the span of centuries we now see that Wolsey's intervention in Lord Percy's wooing of Anne Boleyn not only gained for him the mortal enmity of the lovers whom he separated but made Henry conscious of the subtle hold that his Queen's lady-in-waiting had upon him. Had they been thrown together during those crucial weeks, the fickleness of his lust might have caused him to tire of her. Her absence from Court " for a season " gave his passion no respite and drove him to his fate.

Wolsey also overplayed his hand in speaking disparagingly of the Boleyn family. The son of a butcher he forgot that the aristocrats who surrounded the King despised him. They were forced to curry his favour because he was all-powerful. But they formed a solid block and had their knives ready to plunge into his ribs at the first opportune moment. He should have borne in mind that Anne's father was Sir Thomas Boleyn, son of Sir William Boleyn of Blickling, Norfolk, and of Margaret, daughter and co-heir of Thomas Butler, Earl of Ormond, and that her mother was Lady Elizabeth Howard, the daughter of the renowned Earl of Surrey, afterwards Duke of Norfolk.

Having made the tactical mistake of offending the pride of a woman who felt that she had been denied the privilege of making an advantageous marriage with a man who was most congenial to her, Wolsey soon learnt that the King was determined to make her his bride. In other words, the Cardinal had the conviction thrust upon him that " that certain scrupulosity of conscience " which he had engendered, or at any rate welcomed for reasons of international and dynastic expediency, had become a Frankenstein which threatened to crush him. He saw that with Anne Boleyn installed in the seats of the mighty as Queen of England, the days of his supremacy would be numbered.

The Cardinal was in a sorry quandary. He knew that many difficulties would have to be surmounted before Catherine could be dethroned. He recalled that she was the Aunt of Charles V and could not be treated as a negligible quantity. He considered that it was by no means certain that her marriage to Henry was invalid. But, great as may have been the encouragement that he derived from these factors, he grasped the fact that Anne Boleyn dominated the King's mind and fired his lust and that she and her family were thus able to crush him should he attempt to take up arms against them. He had to deal with the stern reality that the woman whom he had offended had the King's ear.

Wolsey was a practical politician. He saw that

the effect upon his fortunes would be equally disastrous whether Anne Boleyn remained the favourite or became the Queen of Henry VIII. He felt, however, that as long as her hopes were centred upon attaining the sceptre she and her friends would be tempted to make use of his influence at Rome in order to have Catherine's marriage annulled. He thus directed his strategy towards emphasizing what a great man he really was and how, through his offices, the path could be cleared for Henry's union to Anne.

What the Cardinal had in mind was to postpone his day of atonement. A favourite who seeks to become a wife often jeopardizes her influence. She fails to consolidate her power by striving for something greater. When Wolsey became aware that the King was " so amorously affectionate "[1] that his longing for Anne had become an obsession and that she was determined to refuse his embraces unless he made her his consort, he saw a ray of hope for his future. He felt that he had an opportunity to capitalize his vaunted power and to remain in office until the bubble of her influence burst—or until Henry tired of the caprices of his favourite and took another to his heart.

Despite the fact that Francis had given his sister to the King of Navarre on Christmas Day, 1526, and had thus made it impossible for Henry to find an acceptable bride in France, the friendship between Paris and London was then upon such a solid footing

[1] Cavendish, *op. cit.*, p. 204.

that Wolsey did not hesitate to affront Charles V
when the King pressed him, in the spring of 1527,
to come to the relief of his soul by inquiring into the
validity of his marriage with Catherine. We know
what Henry then had in the back of his mind. He,
however, was still a religious man, as far as forms
were concerned, and generally heard " two masses
a day and on holy days High Mass besides." He
thus offered that tribute to virtue which vice so often
pays to it and invoked a motive which spoke solely
of his conscience and said nothing of his passion.

He and Wolsey adopted a most ingenious expedient. The Cardinal was the Legate of the Holy
See. As such he was what canon law calls the
censor morum, or censor of morals. He was the
head of the ecclesiastical courts commissioned to
take cognizance of all matrimonial offences. The
King was cited to appear before him and Archbishop
Warham on May 17th, 1527, " to answer for eighteen
years' sinful cohabitation with Catherine."[1]

The judicial farce set in motion by this citation
was carried out with due solemnity. The Cardinal,
addressing the King, then sitting on his right hand,
explained the reason of the convocation. He set
forth that as it was not fit that a subject should
summon his Sovereign to appear before him he
begged to hear from the King's own lips whether he
consented to these proceedings and was content
that the Archbishop of Canterbury should act as
assessor. Henry answered in the affirmative and

---

[1] Pastor, *op. cit.,* Vol. X, p. 245.

by his reply authorized the Legatine Court to proceed with the business before it.

Wolsey, acting his part in the play, informed the King of the specific complaint made against him, adding " that though a dispensation had been granted him yet as its validity was questioned he ought to feel some scruples of conscience on the subject and dread the vengeance of the Almighty, which sooner or later overtakes those who disobey Him. The Cardinal then demanded from the King what he had to say in justification of this conduct."[1]

The King read his reply from a written paper, the substance of which was that as he could not always appear in person he desired that Dr. John Bell should be recognized as his proctor. This statement was duly registered and the Court prorogued until May 20th. Dr. Bell then appeared and filed a document " containing the King's justification, but admitting the marriage and the impediment."[2]

Wolman, who was technically styled " the promoter of the suit," in due course produced written objections to the King's answer. Bell demanded a copy and the issue was joined. The Bull of Julius II was then offered in evidence. Further proceedings were, however, interrupted because the Court ruled that in a case so intricate canon lawyers and the bishops of the realm should be asked for their considered opinion. This means, to use the phraseology of modern Latin law, that an inquiry or

---

[1] Brewer, *op. cit.*, Vol. II, p. 188.
[2] *Ibid.*, p. 188.

" *enquête* " was ordered. The interlocutory judgment so rendered was not followed by a final decision, for, to quote Brewer, " the proceedings were never resumed."

It is admitted that when this collusive suit was brought before Wolsey and Warham, of which Catherine was not apprised, the King was resolved upon obtaining a divorce at all hazards.[1] He may not have been interested in Anne Boleyn when his conscience first began to prick him about living with the Queen, but when this attempt was made to put Catherine face to face with what diplomatists call a *fait accompli*, lust had already gained the ascendancy over him, although we do not say that he had been permitted to gratify it. A letter sent by him to Anne leaves no doubt about his state of mind at that juncture. He wrote to her :

" If it please you to do the office of a true, loyal mistress, and give yourself, body and heart, to me who have been and mean to be your loyal servant, I promise you *not only the name*, but that I shall make you my sole mistress, remove all others from my affection and serve you only."[2]

We are not inquiring into the secret motives which may or not have actuated Henry or Anne. What we are endeavouring to do is to follow Bishop Burnet's admonition and to adhere to " the reasons which he (the King) always owned, of which all human judicatories must only take notice." And

---

[1] Brewer, *op. cit.*, Vol. II, p. 188.
[2] *Ibid.*, p. 184.

following the official record, as thus made up, we are seeking to ascertain for ourselves what part Clement VII played in this sad chapter in the history of a great people.

Henry and Catherine, and Anne and Wolsey, were all of them Catholics when our narrative opened. The Pope was their spiritual father. They recognized him as such. He may, as a man, have had his own ideas in regard to what Henry really desired and what was the objective envisaged when this collusive suit was brought on May 17th, 1527. But it was his duty, as the supreme head of his Church, to put aside his suspicions and deal with the record as made up in due course of law.

It is thus obvious that the first official phase of the problem with which we are concerned does not present Henry in the attitude of a man who is seeking a divorce. We know what he really wanted. His letter to Anne promised her " not only the name " but that he would make her his " sole mistress " and remove all others from his affection. But he assumed no such attitude at the bar of justice in May, 1527. He appeared there solely as a defendant charged with offending public morals. This is a detail which should not be forgotten.

CHAPTER IV ·

WOLSEY'S EQUIVOCATION

WHEN the Legatine Court met on May 17th, 1527, Wolsey was endeavouring to devise an expedient that would prevent Anne Boleyn and the Norfolk party from ousting him from the King's good graces. He was fighting for his political existence—and also for his neck. He cared no more for Catherine or for her rights or for fundamental justice than he did about climatic conditions at the North Pole. But he was not opposed to her. He was merely indifferent to her fate.

The Cardinal saw in the collusive suit instituted in the name of Wolman an excellent means of keeping his personality in the foreground and of retaining his influence whether Anne was to reign as favourite or as queen. He reasoned that as long as Catherine's marriage remained undissolved Anne would be reluctant to have him thrown overboard through fear that no one else would be able to do as much for her at Rome as he could. He argued that if, after emphasizing all that he had done for her, she finally became the royal Consort, his great services to her would ensure his maintenance in office.

When Wolsey was thus prostituting his intellect

and his prestige for his own selfish ends the Imperial troops, under the Duke of Bourbon, were besieging Rome. A musket-bullet killed that intrepid officer when he was mounting a scaling-ladder planted against the walls of the city. His death unleashed the fury of the Germans, the Spaniards and the Italians in his wake.

" Churches, palaces and the houses of private persons were plundered without distinction. No age, or character or sex was exempt from injury. Cardinals, nobles, priests, matrons, virgins, were all the prey and at the mercy of men deaf to the voice of humanity. . . . Clement, deprived of every recourse and reduced to such extremity of famine as to feed on asses' flesh was obliged to capitulate on such conditions as the conquerors were pleased to prescribe." [1]

Wolsey was so fundamentally both a patriot and an egoist that he at once interpreted this information in the light of England's interests and his personal welfare. He saw that it afforded his country a golden opportunity to come to the fore as the champion of the Pope, to give vital significance to Henry's title of " Defender of the Faith." And he perceived that it gave him an ideal occasion to prove to Anne and the Norfolk party what a great statesman he was and that they could not afford to unhorse him whether she was destined to rule as mistress or reign as consort.

[1] *The History of the Reign of the Emperor Charles V*, by William Robertson, edited by W. H. Prescott, Philadelphia, Lippincott & Co., Vol. II, p. 335.

The entire strategy of the collusive suit had been to manage the whole affair with such complete secrecy that Catherine should know nothing of what was going on until all opportunity for appeal or remonstrance had been excluded. The purpose which Wolsey had in view was that she was to become the victim of legal proceedings in which no plea on her part should be heard, and that she should be condemned by a Tribunal of the King's own choosing, which she could neither challenge nor decline— not unlike the process by which she was afterwards condemned by Cranmer.[1] But the Cardinal, like most men who think that they are inordinately clever, over-reached himself. He forgot that Catherine was bound to hear of the judicial farce which he had attempted to stage.

She did hear of it, and it aroused the fighting blood she had inherited from her parents. She became " very obstinate."[2] She resolved to assert her right to be heard. She demanded that she be represented by counsel.

Wolsey's ingenuity might have found an answer to this demand. He might have fallen back upon the reply that he was hearing this cause as *censor morum* and that it was not within his province to compel Wolman, the " promoter of the suit," to summon her before his bar. But, when the imprisonment of the Pope made it self-evident that the suit could not be rushed to a conclusion, he saw

---

[1] Brewer, Vol. II, p. 189.
[2] *Ibid.*, p. 189.

that Catherine's demand could not be brushed aside unless Francis I was prepared to support him in riding roughshod over her.

The whole structure of the plot, of which Clement obviously knew nothing, had, therefore, to be changed because the Pope had become a prisoner. Francis and Henry, alarmed at the progress of the Imperial arms in Italy, had, even before the taking of Rome, entered into a closer alliance. In order to put a check upon the Emperor's ambition they had agreed to make a vigorous diversion in the Low Countries.

The force of every incentive which had influenced them, at that time, was now increased. To these was added the desire of rescuing the Pope from the Emperor, a motive no less politic than it appeared to be pious. This, however, rendered it necessary to abandon their hostile intentions against the Low Countries, and to make Italy the seat of war, as it was by vigorous operations there they might contribute most effectually towards delivering Rome and setting Clement at liberty.[1]

If the reasons which we have just set forth actuated both Francis and Henry the latter, as Robertson expresses it, " was influenced by one of a most private nature : having begun about this time to form his great scheme of divorcing Catherine of Aragon, towards the execution of which he knew that the sanction of Papal authority would be necessary, he was desirous to acquire as much merit as

[1] Robertson, *op. cit.*, Vol. II, p. 342.

possible with Clement, by appearing to be the chief instrument of his deliverance."[1]

If Henry thus desired to make capital out of the Pope's discomfiture, Wolsey had even stronger personal reasons for working towards the same end. He knew that the Norfolk party disliked him, that Anne hated him because he had spoken disparagingly of her and her family to Lord Percy and that his hold upon his post depended solely upon his making himself indispensable to his Sovereign's passion and to her ambition. We thus find the Cardinal apparently giving his full support not only to the policy common to Francis and Henry but to that which interested his King and Anne.

Politicians whose tenure of office depends upon the fickle favour of those whom they serve dislike absenting themselves from Court. Wolsey felt reasonably certain of his ability to maintain himself in the King's favour as long as he was assured of access to the royal ear. His conceit told him that if hard pressed he could circumvent Anne's machinations provided he could reach Henry without delay.

The Pope's imprisonment made it necessary that he confer with Francis. He was too astute to allow anyone to supplant him. But he feared that while he was away something might happen to permit Anne and the Norfolk faction to undermine his power. He, accordingly, took the precaution of bringing out the fact that during his absence he would consult the canon lawyers and bishops of the

[1] Robertson, *op. cit.*, Vol. II, p. 343.

realm about the validity of Henry's marriage to Catherine. He thus made Henry and Anne feel that the overshadowing reason for his departure was his desire to advance their interests.

This recalls to our minds that the Legatine Court had ordered what modern Latin Law calls an inquiry or " *enquête* " in order to enable Wolsey and Warham to interrogate experts in canon law in regard to the question at issue in the suit brought in defence of public morals. The former delegated himself to accomplish this mission. Brewer, looking at the matter from its practical aspect and not from the standpoint of technical adjective law, says that the Cardinal " was to feel, if possible the pulse of the nation, to discover how the bishops stood affected towards the King's purpose—especially Fisher, the Bishop of Rochester, whose fearless, outspoken opposition, and high reputation for sanctity the King dreaded."[1]

With the political aspects of his mission thus stressed and with emphasis likewise laid upon its importance to the cause that was so dear to the heart of Henry and Anne, Wolsey set out from Westminster on July 3rd, 1527. A plebeian of plebeians he had all the arrogance of an upstart. He had also the dramatic instinct of a stage manager. He believed in playing upon the imagination of the people not only because he enjoyed the limelight of publicity but also because he felt that pomp and ceremony would lend additional prestige to his

[1] Brewer, *op. cit.*, Vol. II, p. 190.

Sovereign's special envoy. It was for this reason that :

"then marched he forward out of his own house at Westminster, passing through all London, over London bridge, having before him of gentlemen a great number, three in a rank, in black velvet livery coats and the most part of them with chains of gold about their necks. And all his yeomen, with noblemen's and gentlemen's servants following him in French tawny livery coats ; having embroidered upon their backs and breasts of the said coats these letters : T. and C., under the cardinal's hat. . . .

"He rode like a Cardinal, very sumptuously, on a mule trapped with crimson velvet upon velvet, and his stirrups of copper and gilt ; and his spare mule followed him with like apparel. And before him he had his two great crosses of silver, the great seal of England, his Cardinal's hat and a gentleman that carried his valance, otherwise called a cloak-bag. . . . Thus passed he through London, and all the way of his journey, having his harbingers passing before to provide lodging for his train."[1]

Wolsey not only attached great importance to the trappings of his equipage but he took special pains to have his suite worthy of so magnificent a setting. "He called before him all his noblemen and gentlemen into his privy chamber ; where they being assembled, he said unto them in this wise in effect :

"' I have called you hither to this intent, to declare unto you that . . . first ye shall understand

---

[1] Cavendish, *op. cit.*, p. 149.

that the King's majesty, upon certain weighty considerations, hath for the more advancement of his royal dignity, assigned me in this journey to be his lieutenant-general ; and what reverence belongeth to the same I will tell you. That for my part I must, by virtue of my commission of lieutenantship, assume and take upon me, in all honours and degrees, to have all such service and reverence as to his highness' presence is meet and due ; and nothing thereof to be neglected or omitted by me that to his royal estate is appurtenant. Therefore, because ye shall not be ignorant in that behalf is one of the special causes of this your assembly, willing and commanding you as entend my favour not to foreget the same in time and place, but every of you do observe this information and instruction as ye will at my return avoid the King's indignation, but to obtain his highness's thanks, the which I will further for you as ye shall deserve.' "[1]

Wolsey knew that his primacy was in jeopardy when he left London on July 3rd, 1527. We have seen that he omitted no precaution which his fertile brain told him could advance his interests. The first night of his journey he lodged at Sir John Wiltshire's where he met Warham, the Archbishop of Canterbury. They conferred about the King's " secret matter."[2] He then pressed on to Rochester where, surrounded by the glamour of his " commission of lieutenantship," he sought to ascertain

---

[1] Cavendish, *op. cit.*, p. 153.
[2] Brewer, *op. cit.*, Vol. II, p. 193.

E

the opinion entertained about that matter by the aged Bishop " reputed the holiest and wisest of " all the clergy of England.[1]

It must not be forgotten that when Wolsey called upon the venerable Fisher he was not only the King's lieutenant-general and a priest and prince of the Catholic Church, but that he was also the presiding judge of the Legatine Court and charged by its interlocutory judgment with the conduct of an inquiry or " *enquête*."   We already know of the general terms of the mandate committed to him. We find, however, that his discharge of his judicial responsibility was not consonant with recognized standards of ethics.   Here are the facts which warrant so severe a stricture :

The Cardinal opened the conversation with Fisher by telling the Bishop that when the King had begun the late negotiations for marrying the Princess Mary to a Prince of the House of France the Bishop of Tarbes had desired to know what had been done " for taking away the impediment of that marriage whereof my lady Princess cometh " and on perusing the bull of dispensation had said that he feared it was not sufficient as the Pope could not dispense in a matter *de jure divino*.

After having thus led up to his theme, Wolsey went on to say that the sole end envisaged by the King was not to insist upon the objections of his marriage with Catherine, but rather to find ways and means, with the advice of those learned in the law,

---

[1] Froude, *op. cit.*, p. 34.

to satisfy the world that the union was valid in the sight of God and man. The Cardinal then added that " Catherine, in her impatience, was hindering the King's thoughtful and benevolent intentions."[1] In a word, he sought, before leaving France, not only to hide the truth from the prelate whose voice carried the greatest weight in England but to lead that influential man into error.

Had Wolsey's discretion been equal to his duplicity he might have left Rochester satisfied that he had won Fisher to his cause. He attempted, however, to insinuate doubts into the Bishop's mind about the validity of the Papal dispensation by weakly combating arguments against it. He soon saw that the saintly old man did not take kindly to his views. The net result of this interview was that he left the next day for Faversham convinced that Fisher could never be induced to certify that the Dispensation was insufficient.

Having completed his " enquête," or more accurately having found out that this mesure d'instruction, if carried out, would be disastrous to the King's cause on account of the moral weight of the opinion of the Bishop of Rochester, the Cardinal soon pressed on to France. " It was believed at the time—and it was the tradition afterwards," writes Froude, " that Wolsey, in his mission to Paris, intended to replace Catherine by a French princess, the more surely to commit Francis to the support of Henry in the divorce and to strengthen the

---

[1] Brewer, op. cit., Vol. II, p. 196.

new alliance. Nothing can be inherently more likely."[1]

If this deduction be justified by the facts it means that Wolsey's duplicity would seem to have been equal to any emergency. When he convened his Legatine Court on May 17th, 1537, and when he left London for France, *via* Rochester, on July 3rd, 1527, he knew that Anne Boleyn and the Norfolk party dominated the King and that his maintenance of his post was dependent upon his ability to please them. We do not know whether Anne was an ambitious woman, a wanton or a tool in the hands of scheming politicians. All that we can safely assert is that at the time upon which our attention is now concentrated she held Henry's heart and Wolsey's fate in the palm of her hand.

Whether the Cardinal went to France resolved to replace Catherine by a French princess or to supplant her by Anne, he appears to have undertaken a mission which envisaged the annulment of Henry's marriage with her who was then Queen of England. Such a procedure, whether a French princess or Anne was to be its eventual beneficiary, was bound to affront Catherine's nephew, Charles V. Wolsey as a statesman, Henry as a man of intelligence, the Norfolk group as politicians and Anne as a woman of the world all saw that unless Francis I gave the King his whole-hearted support in this bold undertaking, it was not feasible.

In view of this it is easy to understand why it

---

[1] Froude, *op. cit.*, p. 41.

CHAPTER V

KNIGHT'S MISSION

CONSISTENCY was not one of Henry's notable characteristics. We know that in the summer of 1527 Anne appealed so strongly to his passion that he was then bent upon divorcing Catherine. We have seen that he was assured by Wolsey that every effort was being made to facilitate the realization of this design. But what the King ardently desired and what he proclaimed to the world were two different things. In a word, he gave out that all that he wanted was an examination into the validity of his marriage with the view of regularizing it and obviating any further objections to the legitimacy of his daughter.[1]

We attach importance to this declaration. It may hide the truth. It may distort the facts. But when knowledge of it reached the Pope, as it unquestionably did, Clement could not retort : " I know that you are both a hypocrite and a liar. You generally hear two masses a day and on holy days High Mass, besides, and yet you are coveting a woman out of wedlock. You are trying to make me

---

[1] Brewer, *op. cit.*, Vol. II, p. 216.

and the English people believe that you are endeavouring to defend your daughter, when I know that
lust and not your paternal instinct is prompting
you." To speak thus was not the Pope's duty. He
had to be guided by the terms of the pleas that
reached him and by the construction that Henry
himself placed upon them.

When Wolsey had completed his mission to
France the second chapter in the inquiry into the
validity of Henry's marriage came to a close. The
first had shown the King in the part of a defendant
with no official intimation on his part of any desire
to annul his union with Catherine. The second
amplifies the significance of this prologue and shows
us that he announced that he intended nothing more
than an examination into the validity of his marriage,
not because "the scrupulosity of his conscience
pricked him" to action, but because, as a father, he
felt constrained to "take away the impediment
of that marriage whereof my lady Princess
cometh."

Wolsey had dominated these two chapters. In
the first, Henry's rôle was a passive one ; in the
second he played a subordinate part. It was he
who opened the third book. We infer, from the
scattered facts which we have culled here and there,
that he and Anne and those who were urging her on
were not satisfied that the Cardinal was acting in
their interests. But Wolsey was known to be a
power in Rome, and they could not afford to fall out
with him any more than they could risk relying upon

him. The King, therefore, decided to send his
secretary, Dr. Knight, to Rome to begin negotiations
with the imprisoned Pope.

Wolsey was not apprised of this mission.[1] He
learnt of it with " ill-disguised dissatisfaction."[2] It
told him that his omnipotence was assailed. It also
informed him that Anne and the Norfolk group did
not consider that it was opportune for them to
declare open war upon him. Had they felt absolutely certain of their ability to get along without him
they would have called for his official—and perhaps
for his literal—decapitation. He thus, while greatly
displeased, felt encouraged to continue his intrigues
in the hope of regaining the undisputed mastery of
the situation.

The Cardinal had conceived an ambitious plan
which, had he been able to carry it through, would
have entrenched him in power. He contemplated
sending to Rome a man in whom he placed implicit
confidence with instructions to obtain a general
mandate for him to have plenary jurisdiction over
the King's suit during the Pope's captivity. A
clause was to be inserted in this general commission,
by virtue of which the Pope would agree in advance
to ratify any sentence pronounced by his vice-
regent.[3] This would have made Wolsey the dictator
of the Catholic Church, as far as England was
concerned, during the entire time that Clement
remained a prisoner.

---

[1] Froude, *op. cit.*, p. 51.
[2] Brewer, *op. cit.*, Vol. II, p. 220.
[3] *Ibid.*, p. 221.

The King and Anne's sponsors understood this just as well as the Cardinal. It did not require any great perspicacity to see through so self-evident a proposition. They knew that if it succeeded Wolsey would be so impregnably ensconced in power that even Henry could be made to feel his authority. They, therefore, did not desire to see the Cardinal invested with greater authority than he already possessed. They were fearful of an expedient that would overshadow the Crown. Knight's secret instructions, accordingly, were to obtain a dispensation for second nuptials, without insisting on a commission for Wolsey.[1]

At a first examination, this move on the part of Henry, Anne and her party appears to be most untimely. We assume that their thoughts were fixed upon the annulment of the marriage with Catherine. A divorce was what they wanted. Why did they begin with the cart before the horse ?

Here is the answer. Anne and those who were interested in keeping her in the foreground, had to be extremely prudent. They were dealing with a man who was most temperamental and who, it is well constantly to recall, " generally heard two masses a day and on holy days High Mass, besides." His background was religious. He thought in terms of theology, or, what is even more important to our subject, he imagined that he did. He could not afford to affront English public opinion. Catherine, as the Venetian Ambassador has already told us, was

[1] Brewer, *op. cit.*, Vol. II, p. 223.

" more beloved by the Islanders than any queen who had ever reigned."

Anne and her partisans were thus forced to let Henry have his way and continue to give out that he intended nothing more than an examination into the validity of his marriage with the view, if possible, of removing all possible irregularities and obviating any future objections to Mary's legitimacy. Had they insisted that Knight should direct his efforts towards annulling Catherine's marriage, Henry might have jumped the traces and got out of hand. They had to permit the King to stress his " scrupulosity of conscience," his paternal instincts and his desire to have an ecclesiastical ruling upon the point that pricked his soul.

There " was method in their madness." Their primary hurdle was the stubborn fact that until this marriage with Catherine was annulled Anne could not be crowned. Whether it was set aside because of proceedings carried on for the purpose of obviating any further objections to Mary's legitimacy or as the result of an action praying for annulment was a matter of academic but not of practical interest. The essential prerequisite, from their point of view, was to have the union with Catherine dissolved so that Anne could be made queen. They, for this reason, allowed the King to have his own way and did not insist that Knight's instructions should interfere with the subterfuge that soothed Henry's conscience and did not throw cold water on his lust.

Anne and her partisans were political strategists

who kept their eye fixed upon their great goal. Henry's misgivings, his desire to have Mary's legitimacy irrevocably established, even his unpromulgated longing for a divorce were all matters of no interest to them unless the annulment of Catherine's marriage put a crown on Anne's head. Their major objective was, accordingly, to make sure that should Henry become free he would automatically, as it were, fall into Anne's arms.

And it was there that he thought by day and dreamt by night of finding refuge. He was, however, too suspicious a man, too much of a theologian, if this form of expression be preferred, to hope for peace of soul in Anne's embraces when his mind was still centred upon those texts of Leviticus which we have already quoted and one of which reads, " And if a man shall take his brother's wife it *is* an unclean thing ; he hath uncovered his brother's nakedness ; they shall be childless." He interpreted this injunction as implying that it was also unlawful for a woman to uncover the nakedness of her sister's husband.

Of course, we do not suggest that Henry had ever married Anne's sister. We read, nevertheless, in Lingard's *History of England*, and other writers agree with him, that :

" To Elizabeth Tailbois, daughter of Sir John Blount, succeeded in the King's affections Mary Boleyn. . . . She retained for some time her empire over the fickle heart of her lover ; but Henry at length treated her as he had treated so many others, and his desertion of Mary furnished, at a subsequent period, a useful lesson to her younger sister, the gay and accomplished Anne Boleyn."[1]

Whether or no lust prompted Henry in coveting Anne's hand his patriotism cannot be challenged. Animal passion may have spurred him on to desire to beget a son by her, but that he desired to have male issue for England's sake, as well as for the physical pleasure of thus serving his country, we take to be incontrovertible. He feared, however, that were he to give himself, body and soul, to Mary Boleyn's sister another text of Leviticus would smite him. He recalled, as we have already seen, that it is also written that :

" For whosoever shall commit any of these abominations even the souls that commit *them* shall be cut off from among their people."

The only way available to Henry to reconcile his craving for Anne with his former relations with Mary and the dreadful penalties decreed by Leviticus was to have the Pope grant him a Dispensation which would cover what he desired. We do not know whether he took any part in drafting the formula that Knight carried to England. We are told by Brewer that it was corrected and recorrected, written and rewritten and that great insistence was laid upon making it sufficiently comprehensive to answer Henry's requirements and Anne's as well.[2]

---

[1] Lingard, *op. cit.*, Vol. IV, p. 474. Strickland, *op. cit.*, Vol. II, p. 535. Pastor, *op. cit.*, Vol. X, p. 241. Burnet and Froude refuse to admit that Mary Boleyn had been Henry's mistress.

[2] Brewer, *op. cit.*, Vol. II, p. 239.

The King appears, at this time, to have had no doubt about the invalidity of his marriage. He composed a treatise elaborating his point of view. The substance of his paper may have been furnished by others, but he laboured assiduously at the work himself and fortified his case with every argument and authority which his reading or ingenuity could supply.[1] " The result was such as might have been anticipated. He convinced himself by his own reasoning ; he believed that no impartial judge could pronounce against him ; he began to look upon every man as an enemy who dared to doubt the success of his cause."[2]

It was because Henry was in this frame of mind, which Anne and the Norfolk faction encouraged, that he put the cart before the horse. He assumed that the law of gravity would propel the vehicle and that what he had to fear was the aftermath, and possibility of his being refused a dispensation to marry Mary Boleyn's sister. Convinced that his freedom from Catherine was a mere formality and looking upon " every man as an enemy who dared doubt the success of his cause," his entire attention was centred upon what he considered to be the crux of the problem confronting him.

All roads may lead to Rome, but Knight soon ascertained, even in those days, that without a passport and a proper *visa* he could not enter the city, still less be allowed an audience with the Pope,

---

[1] Herbert, *op. cit.*, p. 217.
[2] Lingard, *op. cit.*, Vol. IV, p. 492.

who was then a prisoner. Clement's jailer, Charles V, found that it was inconvenient to be the warden of so prominent a potentate. He decided on December 9th, 1527, to allow the Pope to escape and to reach Orvieto in safety. There, with his territory occupied by the Imperial troops, Clement received Knight.

The Pope was obviously most anxious to do everything within his power to oblige the " Defender of the Faith." We have already seen that the future of the Papacy then appeared to be linked to the prestige of England. But Clement had to be prudence personified not only because it was his duty, as head of the Universal Church, to avoid doing anything that savoured of precipitation, but also because he knew that at Orvieto he was still a prisoner of the Imperialists and that Catherine's nephew was their supreme War Lord.

It would appear from Knight's reports to Henry that when the Pope was still confined in the castle of St. Angelo he contrived to send a letter to Knight " to wait in some quiet place and he would send him all the King's requests in as ample a form as they were desired."[1] This missive was probably intercepted by or shown to Clement's jailers and possibly prompted them to let him escape so that they might be able to get a better insight into the relations between their prisoner and Knight by encouraging both of them to believe that they could safely carry on their negotiations.

[1] Froude, *op. cit.*, p. 51.

Be this as it may, it is not suggested that when this letter was sent Clement was aware of the specific terms of Knight's instructions. All that the Pope then knew was that Henry had announced that what he desired was an examination into the legal aspects of his marriage with Catherine, with the view, if possible, of removing any canonical defects that might be latent in it and obviating any further objections to Mary's legitimacy.[1]

It is thus clear that Clement meant that if Knight would wait in some quiet place, " the King's requests " would be complied with, that is to say ways and means would be envisaged looking towards appeasing the " scrupulosity of conscience that pricked " Henry and towards obviating any future objections to Mary's legitimacy. Knight knew, on the other hand, that what the King desired was not to do away with any canonical difficulties that might attach to the marriage with Catherine, but that Henry thought only of holding Anne in his arms at the earliest possible moment.

Knight allowed his enthusiasm to warp his judgment and he misunderstood the Pope's answer, just as Froude and other historians have done. He thought that it meant that Clement was prepared, as the vernacular expresses it, " to sign on the dotted line," overlooking the fact that Clement could not then have known of the King's unexpected wishes or of the terms of the undisclosed instructions.

When the Pope received the King's Secretary in

[1] Brewer, *op. cit.*, Vol. II, p. 216.

audience the formula for the Dispensation which had been prepared in London was submitted to Clement. He did not reject it. On the contrary, he did what a prudent chief of state or a captain of industry would have done under similar circumstances. He referred the document to his legal adviser. Henry, it should be remembered, had proclaimed that his sword was at the disposal of the Papacy. When so powerful and so well disposed a visitor asks for a favour elementary common sense requires that it receive courteous and even sympathetic consideration.

The wish is often father to the thought. Knight imagined that the Pope approved of his request because it was not unceremoniously rejected. He advised his master that all was well. His deductions are, however, offset by his report to the King that Clement turned over the formula " to Cardinal St. Quatuor (Lorenzo Pucci, Cardinal of Santi Quattro) telling him to reform it according to the style of this Court."[1]

The revised Dispensation was dated November 23rd, 1527. Under it, "Henry's Secretary," and here we quote Froude, " obtained something which on examination, proved to be worthless."[2] He was granted a conditional Bull dependent, in so many words, on the proof of the invalidity of the marriage with Catherine. " Before this proof was clearly established, the Bull was absolutely valueless."[3]

[1] Brewer, Vol. II, p. 230.
[2] Froude, p. 52.
[3] Pastor, *op. cit.*, Vol. X, p. 251.

F

Clement's legal adviser, setting to work with the severity of a parliamentary draftsman, had omitted this clause, declared another to be informal, objected to a third as obscure and deleted a fourth as contrary to the policy of the Papacy. Knight, however, was so enamoured of his imaginary success, so gratified at Clement's suavity, so willing to confuse politeness with compliance that he reported to Wolsey: " I do bring a commission with me and a dispensation, which, I trust, the King and your Grace will like well."[1]

Froude's words have already told us that Knight was mistaken. We shall dismiss him from our mind. The salient fact that interests us is that when he returned to London the third phase of Henry's efforts to smother Anne in his embraces had ended without his having taken a single official step towards the annulment of his marriage with Catherine or expressive of an official desire on his part to separate from her.

We may ask ourselves why did Clement and Cardinal St. Quatuor consent to issue the Bull that gratified Knight and " which on examination proved to be worthless " ? Several replies suggest themselves, but the significant one is that this Bull, worthless though it may have been for Henry's purposes, was of the greatest value to the Papacy itself.

We have seen that the challenge to Papal authority was the outstanding peril which menaced the

---

[1] Brewer, *op. cit.*, Vol. II, p. 232.

Catholic Church during Clement's reign. Doctrinal questions did not give to the Greek Schism or to Luther's challenge the driving power which these movements derived from attacking the jurisdiction of the Holy See. It was the assault upon Rome's hegemony that attracted attention.

Henry, in asking the Pope to grant him a Dispensation making it possible for Mary Boleyn's sister eventually to become Queen of England, buttressed the Papal prerogative at a time when Clement's imprisonment lent special emphasis to this recognition. It meant a great deal for the prisoner of Orvieto to receive so striking a tribute from the "Defender of the Faith." Strategic reasons made it imperative that the Pope should take advantage of this exceptional opportunity to proclaim that even his defeat by Charles V did not weaken the spiritual authority of the Papacy. This Bull, from Clement's point of view, was a public demonstration of Papal authority and nothing else.

It was the judicial power of the Church that would eventually be called upon to pass judgment on the point of law raised by Henry's " scrupulosity of conscience." The granting of a Dispensation is an attribute of the executive and not of the judicial authority of the Sovereign. In those days it was considered inconceivable that a King thirty-six years of age, as Henry then was, should live a life of celibacy. All that the Dispensation, as drafted by Cardinal St. Quatuor and issued by Clement, did was to avoid keeping the King in suspense should the ecclesiastical courts eventually rule that his marriage to Catherine had been invalid.

When we consider what it meant to the Papacy, in those trying hours, to have its authority thus attested by England's Monarch and when we remember that it is Froude himself who has already told us that " Henry's Secretary . . . obtained something which on examination proved to be worthless," it strikes us that nothing has as yet come to our attention which would justify us in looking upon Clement VII as a weak and vacillating Pontiff.

CHAPTER VI

ARTHUR'S MAIDEN WIDOW

HENRY persistently maintained that conjugal relations between Catherine and him had ceased since 1524. He was then thirty-three years old and had already had, at least, two mistresses, Elizabeth Blount and Mary Boleyn. His abstention from the Queen's bed must have warned her that he was again straying from the straight and narrow path. When she learned that her consort was contesting the validity of her marriage, she directed the main barrage of her righteous indignation not against the King or Anne Boleyn but against Wolsey.

Catherine appears to have heard, even before Henry appeared in Court on May 17th, 1527, " to answer for eighteen years' sinful cohabitation " with her, that this citation had been served upon him. We say this because Froude records that " Mendoza, writing on the day following the York Place meeting to the Emperor, informed him, as a matter of fact which he had learnt on reliable authority, that Wolsey, for a final stroke of wickedness, was scheming to divorce the Queen."[1]

---

[1] Froude, *op. cit.*, p. 34.

Mendoza was the Spanish Ambassador accredited to the Court of Saint James. It was to him, as her nephew's representative, that Catherine had appealed when the conviction was forced upon her that the King was seeking to get rid of her. We see, from the substance of the envoy's language, that he and the Queen associated the Cardinal with " this final stroke of wickedness " and that they looked upon him as the instigator of the trouble.

There is something uncanny about the intuition of a woman. It often defies all canons of logic, all rules of evidence, and even all principles of fair play, but, somehow or other, it frequently arrives at objective truth just as well, if not more accurately, than the most painstaking investigations of the most intelligent and impartial and best informed of men. We are led to make this general observation because Pastor, the Austrian Professor whose monumental and authoritative *History of the Popes* is a model of scholarship and a mine of research, proclaims that :

" Behind her (Anne Boleyn) stood two members of the great English nobility ; her uncle, the Duke of Norfolk, and the Duke of Suffolk. . . . From this quarter came the notion of a divorce ; the idea itself originated in a subtly contrived plan to over-throw the all-powerful Chancellor. Should the divorce and the marriage with Anne succeed, the downfall of the Cardinal would follow upon them ; if they did not succeed, then Wolsey would incur the King's wrath on account of their miscarriage, so that in either case the fall of the hated favourite seemed certain. In entire contradiction to the facts is the theory, at one time often upheld, that Wolsey, who was at first antagonistic, had, against his better conscience, and to his own undoing, consented to become the King's tool in carrying out the business, and was the originator of the scheme of divorce."[1]

We prefer to be guided, in this instance, by the intuition of the Spanish woman rather than by the learning of the Austrian professor. The evidence adduced by him does not, in our opinion, support the judgment which he has rendered *ex-cathedra*. It is a hazardous thing for a man to assail the infallibility of a woman's intuition, and Pastor uses reasoning rather than evidence to support his rejection of Catherine's theory.

We have just seen that Mendoza reported to Charles V that " Wolsey, for a final stroke of wickedness, was scheming to divorce the Queen." We should underscore the words " *final stroke* " for they give us the clue to the problem with which we are now confronted.

The orientation of the foreign policy of Henry VII had been towards cementing the relations between England and Spain. This is why he had betrothed his two sons, first Arthur and then Henry, to Catherine, the daughter of Ferdinand and Isabella. The corollary to this was that he was opposed to the hegemony of France. When, with the march of events, Spain became the dominant power in Europe

[1] Pastor, *op. cit.*, Vol. X, p. 242.

and, we may add in the world, Wolsey saw that
" the proper balance on the Continent, to which
England owed both her safety and importance would
be entirely lost "[1] if London backed Valladolid
against Paris. He, accordingly, sought to foster the
friendship of the House of Valois and to isolate the
Spanish dynasty.

Such political strategy, born of patriotism, was
anathema to Mendoza. He considered that it
savoured of wickedness. The Cardinal thought of
alliances in terms of men and women. We have
seen that he endeavoured to find a French Consort
for Princess Mary. What is more logical than that,
contemplating with horror the civil wars that would
menace England should Henry die without male
issue, and observing that the King's superstitions
were aroused by the maledictions contained in
Leviticus, he should seek to capitalize this obsession
and persuade Henry to divorce Catherine and wed a
French Princess? It must be remembered that
Wolsey was far more of a statesman than a priest.

This deduction accounts for Mendoza's reference
to a " final stroke of wickedness " for, from his point
of view, it was the consummation of a policy that
foretold a close working alliance between France
and England. It also explains the attitude of
Norfolk and Suffolk who were the Cardinal's rivals.

They felt that two could play at the same game.
They found in Anne a postulant for Henry's
affections. The King's lust gained the ascendancy

[1] Robertson, *op. cit.*, Vol. II, p. 274.

over higher politics. Wolsey became alarmed and tried to back water. The momentum of the ship of state had, however, become too great. He could not turn back. He had to steer towards the eventual harbour of divorce although he, no doubt, hoped, by careful tacking, to win the King over to a political marriage before port was reached. At all events it was in his interests to get rid of Catherine.

It is not improbable that we, too, may be mistaken, and that Wolsey and he alone may be the villain of the piece. And, after all, the sole question with which we are now concerned is Catherine's point of view. She was convinced that the Cardinal was the arch criminal. She feared that he might deliver judgment against her as Papal Legate.[1] We thus find her, through Mendoza, instructing the Emperor that,

" it would be very advisable, if, with all possible secrecy, the Pope were put upon his guard in case any application should be made to Rome unfavourable to the marriage ; also that his Holiness should tie the Legate's hands and, by having the cause transferred entirely to himself, prevent the Legate from taking part in it or appointing judges for it in this country."[2]

Not content with seeking to deprive Wolsey of judicial authority to inquire into the validity of her marriage, Catherine spoke to Henry about this attempt to annul their union. He replied that they

---

[1] Froude, *op. cit.*, p. 35.
[2] Brewer, *op. cit.*, Vol. II, p. 203.

had been living in mortal sin and that a separation was necessary. She refused to admit the charge. He retorted that, after questioning various theologians and canonists, their adulterous relations did not brook discussion. She answered that " even if it were granted that serious objections might be raised against the Papal Dispensation permitting a marriage with the wife of a deceased brother, yet, in her case, they could not apply, for, as her husband well knew, she had been Arthur's wife only in name, for their marriage had never been consummated.[1]"

This affirmation, which Henry did not then controvert, appears to have completely changed the legal strategy of those who were endeavouring to deprive Catherine of her crown. It made it necessary for them to consult their theologians and canonists and to examine the matter from a new angle. All parties opposed to the Queen had taken for granted that Arthur had had carnal knowledge of Catherine. Her categorical refutation of this assumption, coupled with Henry's tacit admittance that she had spoken the truth, caused them to return to their law books and to revise their plan of campaign.

This put an end to what we may describe as the fourth phase of Henry's inquiry into the validity of his marriage. We have not yet found him in the part of a plaintiff suing for the annulment of his union. We now see him in the light of a man

---

[1] Pastor, *op. cit.*, Vol. X, p. 246.

" whose scrupulosity of conscience had been pricked " but who, when told by Catherine that " she was a true maid without touch of a man "[1] when first he held her in his arms, asked himself whether the Levitical penalty really applied to his case.

It is not improbable that, confronted with Catherine's assurances, Henry might have found a way of gratifying his passionate longing for Anne without making her his queen, if it had not suited Wolsey's conception of international politics, and the Norfolk party's desire to overthrow the Cardinal, for both of them to vie with one another in keeping the King's mind centred upon his superstitious fears. The Cardinal could not afford to falter because, had he done so, Anne might have whispered in the monarch's ear that the priest was a traitor whose neck should be severed. Norfolk and Suffolk had too valuable a political pawn in Anne's sex-appeal to let the matter lag.

The interview between Henry and Catherine took place before Wolsey had left for France. The Cardinal's fertile mind, stimulated in its activity by the fear that he might be decapitated should the King think that he was not a divorce enthusiast, found an answer to the question raised by the Queen. He said that even if the marriage with Arthur had never been consummated, the fact still remained that they had been married " *in facie ecclesiæ.*" This established, he went on to say, the impediment

[1] Cavendish, *op. cit.* p. 215.

of open wedlock from which the Papal Bull gave no valid Dispensation.   Therefore, he continued, the invalidity of the King's marriage could be asserted, even in the teeth of the Queen's assertion, for the reason that the Dispensation had been insufficient.[1]

We see from this reply, that the Cardinal had his line of attack more or less elaborated before he left London for Paris.   Attention has been called to the circumstance that the King, preferring not to rely entirely on Wolsey, had sent Knight to Rome with instructions of which the Cardinal had heard with " ill-disguised dissatisfaction."   We shall not repeat what has already been said about the failure of this mission, but pass on to the attitude adopted by Wolsey in the face of Henry's tacit admission that Catherine came to his couch a virgin.

We remarked that Wolsey had argued that as Catherine and Henry had been married *in facie ecclesiæ* " the invalidity of the King's marriage could be asserted, even in the teeth of the Queen's assertion, for the reason that the Dispensation had been insufficient."   We have not forgotten that Henry himself had originally " written of it that he found it (his marriage) was unlawfull, *de Jure divino* and *undispensable*."[2]

There was a perfectly sound reason, based upon a knowledge of human psychology, which prompted Wolsey, the man of affairs, in taking this attitude. It was not a case of sacrificing the interests of the

---

[1] Pastor, Vol. X, p. 247.
[2] Herbert, *op. cit.*, p. 217.

King to add to the prestige of the Pope. Burnet
goes to the root of the matter when he writes :

" It would have been unacceptable to have
insisted on the nullity of the bull . . . because the
matter of it was unlawful, and fell not within the
Pope's power. For Popes, like other princes, do
not love to hear the extent of their prerogatives
disputed or defined. And, to condemn the Bull of
a former Pope as unlawful, was a dangerous pre-
cedent at a time when the Pope's authority was
rejected by many in Germany. Therefore the
canonists, as well as divines, were consulted to find
such nullities in the Bull of Dispensation as according
to canon law, and the proceedings of the Rota,
might serve to invalidate it without any diminution
of the Papal power."[1]

Wolsey showed excellent judgment in following
this line of attack. It emphasized the Papal prerogative " at a time when the Pope's authority was
rejected by so many in Germany." It gained for
Henry a measure of personal sympathy which was
all the greater at a moment when Rome had just
been sacked by the Imperial troops, when Clement
had not yet " escaped " from St. Angelo and when
virtual imprisonment at the hands of Catherine's
nephew still awaited him at Orvieto.

When the canonists examined the Bull which
Julius II had issued authorizing Catherine to marry
Henry they found in it many points upon which
to base their arguments. There is nothing

---

[1] Burnet, *op. cit.*, Vol. I, p. 62.

mysterious about law, however impenetrable its
terminology may often appear to be.   It is organized
common sense.   It has its rules of the game, just
as cricket or bridge.   One of these is that fair play
must dominate the relations between men.   It is in
application of this principle, that Burnet declares in
his *History of the Reformation* that it is a maxim of
canon law " that if the Pope be surprised in
anything, and Bulls be procured upon false
suggestions and untrue premises, they may be
annulled afterwards."[1]

Taking their cue from this salutary rule Henry's
canonists held that Julius II had been led to grant
the Dispensation upon an inaccurate statement of
facts.   Their first argument revolved around the
King's age when the Bull was applied for and granted.
He was then not yet in his teens.   He had not
reached the age of puberty, as fixed by canon law.
He was thus a minor and as such unable to formulate
a wish.   The preamble of the Dispensation sets forth
that Henry—not his father Henry VII, but Henry,
the Prince of Wales—" desired that he might be
dispensed with to marry the Princess."[2]

This was false, said these canonists, for the King
had not validly expressed such a desire being then
a minor and unable to do so.

The next point which Henry's battery of theologians brought forward was that the preamble
declared that the Bull was desired by Henry in

---

[1] Burnet, *op. cit.*, Vol. I, p. 62.
[2] *Ibid.*, p. 62.

order to preserve the peace between the King of England and Ferdinand and Isabella. They held that no boy of twelve could possibly have thought along such lines and that the conceptions attributed to him were obviously a pure fabrication. They went further and pointed out that England and Spain were at peace when the application for the Bull was made and when it was issued and that there were no war clouds upon the horizon which required that exceptional measures be then taken to preserve the peace between these two countries.

And stressing this argument still further they held that as the King of England referred to in the Bull, Henry VII, and Isabella of Spain also designated in it, were both dead when the marriage took place, it " could not be made valid by virtue of a Bull that was granted to maintain amity between them that were dead before the marriage was consummated."[1]

The canonists next seized upon the fact that when Henry became of age he had protested against the representations made in his name. This step, they held, " did retract any such pretended desire that might have been made in his name." Driving home this argument they went on to say that " any pretended desire before he was of age being clearly annulled and determined by that protestation after he was of age . . . a subsequent marriage founded upon the Bull must needs be void."[2]

[1] Burnet, *op. cit.*, Vol. I, p. 63.
[2] *Ibid.*, p. 63.

When these various criticisms of the Dispensation had been thus elaborated, Wolsey appears to have advised Henry that they were the grounds along which the canonists deemed that the litigation should be carried on at Rome. The Cardinal's inquiry or *enquête* had already told him that Fisher of Rochester, as the mouthpiece of English public opinion, would stand in the way of confronting Catherine with a judgment rendered in a collusive suit. It was, accordingly, obvious both to Wolsey and Henry that they had, as Burnet expresses it, " to put the matter home to the Pope."[1]

We find, therefore, as we bring this stage of our investigation to a close that the eyes of Catherine, Henry, Wolsey, Norfolk and Anne were all turned towards Rome. Catherine sought to have Clement curtail the Cardinal's Legatine authority ; Wolsey to have it enlarged ; and Henry, Norfolk and Anne, buoyed by the King's conviction that his marriage was invalid and its annulment merely a question of time, thought primarily of obtaining from the Pope a Dispensation that would permit Anne, Mary Boleyn's sister, to share the royal couch, not as mistress but as wife.

Burnet, *op. cit.*, Vol. I, p. 71.

CHAPTER VII

CASALI'S MANDATE

WOLSEY did not make the mistake of under-estimating the difficulties which confronted him. He did not, like Henry, " look upon every man as an enemy who dared to doubt the success of his cause." He did not send to Rome an English official who knew nothing of the by-paths of Vatican diplomacy. On the contrary, conscious of the fact that his political future, and, perhaps, his head were in jeopardy he followed a custom which was by no means uncommon in those days. He committed his interests and the King's cause to an Italian,[1] Sir Gregory Casali or Casalis, then ordinary English Ambassador at Rome.[2]

The instructions given to this plenipotentiary are in Latin. They are dated December 5th, 1527, and cover fifteen and a half closely printed pages. They declare that the King had found " that he could no longer, with a good conscience, continue in that marriage with the Queen, having God and

---

[1] Herbert, *op. cit.*, p. 217.
[2] Burnet, *op. cit.*, Vol. I, p. 71. An anonymous author in the January, 1877, *Quarterly Review*, tells us that " for the delicate mission of inducing the Pope to abdicate his supreme functions in Wolsey's hands, he had chosen to employ none but Italians."

the quiet and salvation of his soul chiefly before his eyes."[1]   They specifically mention that Henry " looked on the death of his sons as a curse from God."   They go on to say that " to avoid further judgments he now desired the help of the Apostolic See, to consider his case . . . and to find a way that he, being divorced from the Queen, may marry another wife, of whom by the blessing of God, he might hope for male issue."[2]

When Casali was given this mandate Clement VII was still a prisoner at St. Angelo.   The Ambassador was instructed " to make a condolence of the miseries the Pope and the Cardinals were in, . . . and to assure the Pope that they (Henry and Wolsey) would use all the most effectual means that were possible for setting him at liberty . . . as if there were no other way to come to the Kingdom of Heaven but by doing it. . . . And," continued the Cardinal, " because money was like to be the most powerful argument, especially to men impoverished by a captivity, ten thousand ducats were remitted to Venice, to be distributed as the King's affairs required ; and he was empowered to make farther promises as he saw cause for, which the King would faithfully make good."

---

[1] The full text of the Instructions are contained in Vol. II of Burnet's *History of the Reformation*.   The excerpts in our text are taken from Burnet's translation given in Vol. I of the same work.

[2] It will have been observed that Casali was not instructed to petition the Pope to annul Henry's marriage with Catherine.   Another procedure would appear to have been contemplated for that purpose.   What the Ambassador was directed to do was to obtain the help of the Apostolic See to find a way so that Henry " being divorced from the Queen, may marry another wife."

Wolsey was particularly anxious to have Casali attempt to corrupt Lorenzo Pucci, Cardinal of Santi Quattro.[1] The reason for this special emphasis placed upon bribing that prelate was that he was the legal adviser to whom the Pope had referred the Draft Dispensation brought to Orvieto from London by Knight. Wolsey hoped to circumvent Clement's prudence by suborning his right-hand man. His instructions carried this detail:

" Endeavour to have a private audience with the Cardinal and find out adroitly what will best seduce him. Let me know, as soon as possible, if his heart longs for costly apparel, vases of gold or horses. I shall arrange matters to prove to him that he is dealing with a prince who is neither cruel nor ungrateful."

Wolsey did not content himself with sending these orders to Casali. He also transmitted a Commission which had been prepared in London and which he desired that the Pope should accept unaltered. It was obvious that this draft would be submitted to Lorenzo Pucci, Cardinal of Santi Quattro, and this is why Wolsey attached such importance to corrupting him.

The Commission, which it was sought to have Clement accept without alteration, began with this preamble:

" Whereas eighteen years ago, our dearest son in Christ, Henry VIII, King of England, etc., was

---

[1] Various authors spell this name in different ways. The same remark applies to Casali's name.

induced by the permission of those about him and a pretended Apostolic Dispensation to contract marriage with Catherine, his brother's widow and

" Whereas it has been found, upon further examination, that the said Dispensation was granted on false pretences, and is faulty and surreptitious, that thereby the King's conscience is troubled ; and that, in full confidence of our supreme ruler here on earth,

" he has required, etc., etc."[1]

After having laid down these various predicates, this Commission, which Wolsey hoped to have Clement accept by bribing the Papal *Contentieux* or law staff, continues in these words :

" In consideration of the premises we appoint you our dear son, the Cardinal of York, of whose virtues, love of justice and equity, we are well assured, to exercise our authority in your own person for the trial of this cause. We also appoint you . . . . as assessor, enacting that the decision of either of you shall be valid in the absence of the other.

" You are to proceed summarily and *de pleno*, without the publicity or formality of judicial proceedings, and inquire into the validity of this Dispensation. And if you, jointly or severally, are satisfied of its invalidity, you shall pronounce the marriage between Henry and Catherine to be null and void, allowing the parties to separate and contract marriage *de novo*, all appeals or challenge set aside.

[1] Brewer, *op. cit.*, Vol. II, p. 236.

" Also by this, our authority, we empower you to overrule all canonical defects or objections, and declare the issue of the first as well as of the second marriage to be legitimate. And whatever is done by you in this cause, judicially or extra-judicially, we ratify and confirm in the fullest manner, without revocation."[1]

So confident was Wolsey that he could do what he wanted at Orvieto or Rome by presenting to the Cardinal of Santi Quattro " costly apparel, vases of gold or horses " that he unobtrusively inserted in his instructions to Casali these lines :

" I send you a Dispensation, also drawn in due form of a Brief, to be expedited by his Holiness affixing to it his signature and seal. And though the King does not fear any consequences that might possibly ensue, yet, remembering from the example of past times what fictitious claims have been put forward, to cut off all controversy for the time to come, he requests this of the Pope, as a thing absolutely necessary."[2]

Before we speak of the Commission which Wolsey hoped to receive let us say a few words about this Dispensation to which he so artfully referred. We already know its terms. It was a second attempt to obtain what Knight had failed to get. Its purpose was to permit Henry to marry Anne, because, says an anonymous author in the *Quarterly Review*, " the King had been the lover of her mother and her

---

[1] Brewer, *op. cit.*, Vol. II, p. 236.
[2] *Ibid.*, p. 238.

sister."[1]   There is no proof whatsoever that he had
ever been the lover of her mother.   This proposed
Bull, while thus envisaging Henry's relations with
Mary Boleyn and nobody else, was desired in order
to permit him to marry Anne[2]   It shows that he
was still dominated by her, that his superstitions
continued to master him and that he was afraid to
marry her without a Dispensation.

When these made-in-England Commission and
Dispensation were submitted to Clement by Casali
he turned them over to his law officer, that is to
say to the Cardinal whom Wolsey had sought to
bribe.   The ruling was made that a Commission
so drawn could not pass without perpetual dishonour
to the Pope, the King and the Cardinal.[3]

Wolsey must have foreseen this result for, finding
that his attempted bribery appeared to be foredoomed
to failure, he told Casali to resort to menaces.   The
Commission had spoken of " our plenary power as
supreme ruler here on earth " and had burnt incense
to Papal authority.   The Cardinal thought that, with
Clement a prisoner at Orvieto, such language would
obtain for Henry anything and everything.
Following up this point he wrote to Casali :

" His Majesty will of two evils choose the least ;
and as he is absolutely resolved to satisfy his con-

---

[1] *Quarterly Review, op. cit.,* p. 18.   Burnet, in his *History of the
Reformation,* Vol. I, p. 64, refutes a story first given publicity about
eighty years after Henry's death to the effect that the wife of Sir
Thomas Boleyn had been his mistress and that Anne Boleyn was the
fruit of their adultery.   The story is as false as it was malicious.
[2] Brewer, *op. cit.,* Vol. II, p. 239.
[3] *Ibid.,* p. 237.

science, if, in so doing, he cannot obtain redress from the Holy See, he will cease to respect it and its authority will fall into contempt from day to day, especially in these perilous times."[1]

Neither the " ten thousand ducats (which) were remitted to Venice, to be distributed as the King's affairs required " or " the farther promises . . . which the King would faithfully make good," these menaces or the proposition to have the desired Commission made out in the name of Cardinal Staffileo, Dean of the Rota, were able to obtain for Wolsey what he wanted.

Casali reported to his Chief that he found the Pope at Orvieto miserable and alone, irresolute and dispirited.[2] Whatever may have been Clement's physical and mental condition he did not blindly sign what was placed before him. He had the documents passed upon by his legal staff and accepted them as re-drafted and not as tendered. The teeth were extracted from them and the venom removed. When Henry and Wolsey went over them in London they were deemed to be unsatisfactory for their purposes.

The radical difference between the Commission submitted by Casali to the Pope and the one signed was that the latter omitted the very feature on which Wolsey set the greatest value. It deleted the declaration that the five points laid down, if substantiated, would suffice to annul the marriage.

[1] Brewer, *op. cit.*, Vol. II, p. 237.
[2] *Ibid.*, p. 241.

It did away with the possibility of a final decision being taken in England. It made worthless the plenary powers conferred on Wolsey.[1]

The statements of fact which have so far been set forth in this chapter are based upon official documents made readily accessible to us largely through Brewer's indefatigable industry. We have now reached a stage in our narrative where source material fails us and where we have to consider two serious charges brought against Clement VII, by writers whose names command general respect. One affects his moral courage, the other his personal honour. Moral cowardice in a Sovereign may be as reprehensible as any vice. Both attacks thus deal with matters of the utmost importance.

The first portrays the Pope as the personification of pusillanimity, as a Monarch who apologised for doing his duty, as a Pontiff who sought a pretext for facing the responsibilities of his exalted trust.

He is pictured as having beseeched Knight, with "many sighs and tears," to refrain from letting the world know anything of that valueless Dispensation of which we spoke in the preceding chapter. We are told that he suggested that Henry should have Lautrech with the French army push forward and, "coming where the Pope" was, insist upon the immediate issuance of that Dispensation so that Clement could say to Charles : " I refused to sign this Bull when it was presented to me by the English

---

[1] Pastor, *op. cit.*, Vol. X, p. 254.

Ambassador. I had to yield when he backed up his demand by the sword of the General of the French army."[1]

News items which appear in certain metropolitan journals are sometimes characterized as " important if true." Such a remark applies to this assault upon Clement's reputation. The indictment is launched, repeated and broadcast, but it is not substantiated by creditable source material.

Burnet's *History of the Reformation*, which we have just given as our authority for this most grave accusation, is a most valuable book of reference on account of the " Collection of Records and Original Papers and other Instruments," which supplement its text. Its margins are surcharged with notes. Not one of them, in this instance, informs us who, in the final analysis, vouches for this serious attack upon the reputation of Clement VII.

Herbert, whose *Life and Raigne of King Henry the Eighth* was published in 1649, and who, according to the *Encyclopædia Britannica*, "judges the character and statesmanship of Henry with too obvious partiality,"[2] is probably the author upon whom Burnet relies for his information. He begins by offering a somewhat different version of the soft impeachment. He portrays not Clement but Lorenzo Pucci Cardinal Sanctorum Quatuor as " earnestly intreating our King neverthelesse not to put it (the Dispensation) in execution till the

---

[1] Burnet, Vol. I, p. 75 (the substance not the exact words).
[2] *Encyclopædia Britannica*, XIII Edition, Vol. XIII, p. 341 C.

Spaniards and the Almains were gone out of Italie, and himself left in full libertie."[1]

Herbert then adds : "moreover he (Lorenzo Pucci Cardinall Sanctorum Quatuor) tells (as in the Pope's name) that if *Monsieur de Lautrech* were come, the Pope thinketh he might, by good Colour, say to the Emperour, that he was required by the English Ambassadours and *Monsieur de Lautrech* to proceed in the businesse."[2] A letter from Knight to Wolsey, dated Orvieto, January 1st, 1528, confirmed by a dispatch from Casali to Wolsey, of January 13th, 1528, is invoked by Herbert to justify his statements.

Burnet, Brewer, Froude and other authors assert that after Casali had obtained from the Pope the Commission and the Dispensation to which we have referred he was informed by " the Pope and the Cardinals,"[3]

" that either by virtue of the Commission that the Secretary had obtained, or by the Legatine power that was lodged with the Cardinal of York, he (Henry) should proceed in the business. And if the King found the matter clear in his own conscience . . . he should without more noise make judgment be given; and presently marry another wife, and then send a Legate to confirm the matter. And it would be easier to ratify all when it was once done, than to go on in a process from Rome. . . . If the thing went on in England, and the King had once married

---

[1] Herbert, *op. cit.*, p. 218.
[2] *Ibid.*, p. 218.
[3] Froude, *op. cit.*, p. 63.

another wife, the Pope would find very good reasons to justify the confirming a thing that was gone so far."[1]

The only proof that is proffered, as far as we know, in support of this latter most damning accusation, which manifestly challenges Clement's good faith, is the report sent by Casali to Wolsey dated January 13th, 1528, to which we have already referred. At all events, this is the only evidence adduced by Burnet and Froude. Brewer, who is usually so meticulously careful and who almost invariably supports his text by adequate quotations, in this particular instance does not enable us to control what he has affirmed. We thus have Knight and Casali as the only witnesses for the prosecution known to us in support of charges which affect the moral courage and the personal honour of the Pope.

Both accusations are so intimately interwoven that we shall deal with them as if they were but two phases of one and the same bill of particulars. In the light of the facts available to us we deny that the Pope used any such language as that imputed to him by either Knight or Casali. We consider the reports submitted by them to the King and the Cardinal as unblushing falsehoods.

Before our counter-attack be brushed aside as being nothing but a convenient device for striking out of the record evidence which cannot be refuted we ask that the following facts be recalled :

(1) Knight and Casali were sent to Italy to

---

[1] Burnet, *op. cit.*, Vol. I, p. 77.
See also Brewer, *op. cit.*, Vol. II, p. 243.

accomplish a delicate mission, the success or failure of which was a matter of vital importance not only to them but to their principals ;

(2) Their reports are contemporaneous documents, dated respectively January 1st and January 13th, 1528 ;

(3) They were at Orvieto at the same time, the former representing the King, the latter the Cardinal ;

(4) Ten thousand ducats had been remitted to Venice to be distributed as the King's affairs required ;

(5) Casali was empowered to make " farther promises, as he saw cause for, which the King would faithfully make good " ;

(6) Casali had received the following specific instructions from Wolsey : " Endeavour to have a final audience with the Cardinal (Lorenzo Pucci Cardinal Santi Quattro) and find out adroitly what will best seduce him. Let me know, as soon as possible, if his heart longs for costly apparel, vases of gold or horses " ;

(7) Agents who accept orders to corrupt officials of a foreign government, prince or potentate invariably collect the cash placed at their disposal for the purposes of executing their mission ;

(8) They cannot and do not obtain receipted vouchers for the sums disbursed by them and thus do not furnish their principals with written evidence that they have actually used the cash which has come into their hands ;

(9) Whether Casali did or did not embezzle the money, in whole or in part, placed at his disposal by Wolsey, it cannot be denied that he had assumed the task of obtaining the Commission and the Dispensation desired by his principals;

(10) We have no evidence before us that Knight had, under his control, any funds intended for corruption purposes, but he had manifestly accepted a mandate not to come back to England without the documents called for by his Master;

(11) Both Casali and Knight failed in their undertakings;

(12) They knew, when their two reports were dispatched to London, that they had not succeeded;

(13) It is logical to suppose that, face to face with the stubborn facts that both of them had failed and that both of them would be censured because of their failure, they compared notes and invented the tales which we know in order to be able to say:

"Of course we have succeeded. The best proof that Knight obtained what the King had commissioned him to get is found in the fact that the Pope is afraid to let the world know that the Dispensation is substantially what was asked for; indisputable evidence that Casali's brain produced a brilliant coup is shown by the way in which the Pope told him how the King could marry Anne without loss of time."

Had any such immoral suggestion been made to Casali by the Pope or by any high official of the

Papacy as that referred to in this report of January 13th, 1528, we would have seen some evidence of its having been followed up by Henry or Wolsey. We would have found an indication of an attempt having been made then and there to take advantage of the opening offered by such advice. The King and his Minister were not men to throw away golden opportunities. Norfolk and Anne had too much at stake to permit them to do so even if they had been so inclined.

Far from discovering proof of any such activity on the part of anybody, far from finding Casali high in favour for having gained so signal an advantage, we see in the fact that upon the receipt of their reports he and Knight were superceded by two other emissaries, Fox and Gardiner, proof that neither the King nor the Cardinal, Norfolk or Anne believed a word of these two dispatches. If they did not, why should we ? If they did, why did they then and there do nothing to take advantage of the invaluable suggestion submitted by the Italian who had handled their money ?

We are convinced that an Anglo-Saxon jury would not convict a man upon the evidence which we have before us unless concomitant circumstances and the test of cross-examination had satisfied it that Knight and Casali had told the truth. These two emissaries had so great an interest in defaming Clement and Lorenzo Pucci that their testimony is open to grave suspicion. They sought to bolster up their impaired prestige, to save their face, as the

Chinese would put it, by attacking the Pope and his advisers. We are afraid that many an historian has taken their word as true without submitting it to the proper test and utterly oblivious of the injustice thus done to Clement and the Papacy. Popes and Cardinals are men and as such are entitled to fair play.

We read in Burnet's *History of the Reformation* that " in this whole matter, the Pope carried himself as a wise and politic prince that considered his interest and provided against dangers with great foresight."[1] This statement immediately follows his assertion, supported solely by the testimony of the unsuccessful corruptionist, Casali, that : " the Cardinal Sanctorum Quatuor got four thousand crowns as the reward of his pains and in earnest of what he was to expect when the matter should be brought to a final conclusion."

When so stout a champion of Henry and such a redoubtable opponent of Catholicism gives Clement such an encomium after speaking so disparagingly of the chief legal officer of the Papacy, who, we know, refused to do the bidding of the King or the Cardinal, it appears to us that we are justified in refusing to believe that the Pope was either a moral coward or a dishonourable man. At all events, we are constrained to hold that the facts so far reviewed in these pages signally fail to substantiate the attacks made upon him.

[1] Burnet, *op. cit.*, Vol. I, p. 76.

CHAPTER VIII

FOX AND GARDINER

BEFORE we follow Fox and Gardiner, as they make their way to Orvieto in their attempt to carry out the mission which Knight and Casali had failed to execute, let us pause, for an instant, and consider what it would have meant to Henry had the reports submitted by these two unsuccessful emissaries not ~~have~~ been a tissue of falsehoods. We know that Wolsey was definitely committed, in January, 1528, to do the King's bidding even if he had to prostitute his honour in order to do so. We also have not forgotten that Henry's longing for Anne then took the shape of an all-consuming passion.

This does not mean that we hold that lust engendered " that scrupulosity that pricked the King's conscience " and caused him to inquire into the validity of his marriage with Catherine. We know that to a certain school of thought it is essential that the scruples of Henry should have preceded the proposals of marriage made by him to Anne Boleyn.[1] All that we affirm is that as early as the summer of 1527, his passion so swayed his mind that

---

[1] *Quarterly Review*, January, 1877, *op. cit.*, p. 13.

he wrote letters to his " own sweetheart "[1] which have been described as " more remarkable for their freedom than their refinement."[2]

When a man at the zenith of his animal attributes so far forgets his restraint as to write amorous notes of such a type to a woman young enough to be his daughter and whose passionate nature he considers vouched for by his carnal knowledge of her sister, his entire being is dominated by a single thought. He is prepared to sell his soul to possess her. Had Henry, a prey to such lustful longing, believed that Clement had ever said to Casali that he (the King) " should without more noise make judgment be given and presently marry another wife, and then send for a legate to confirm the matter "[3] he and Anne would have acted upon the spur of the moment, instructed Wolsey to convene the Legatine Court, pronounce judgment and marry them without the loss of a precious moment. These orders would have been obeyed.

Casali was a nimble-witted Italian, but not a canonist. He had not been informed that canon law has its rules of procedure, that they are well known to theologians and that the proposal he attributed to Clement was a manifest absurdity. It was a transparent juridical heresy patent to both Henry and Wolsey. They saw at once that without a specific Bull emanating from the Pope and conferring extraordinary powers upon the Legatine Court, its

[1] Brewer, *op. cit.*, Vol. II, p. 245.
[2] *Ibid.*, p. 207.
[3] Burnet, *op. cit.*, Vol. I, p. 77.

H

decision would not be executory until ratified by the Holy See.

It was rank nonsense for Casali to put into the mouth of Clement the words we have quoted because the King and the Cardinal were fully aware that any judgment that might be handed down in England, as the law then stood, would remain inchoate until confirmed by the Supreme Pontiff. We thus find the entire strategy of Fox and Gardiner directed to establishing what Casali, in his blissful ignorance, had assumed to be axiomatic. This will become self-evident as we follow the arguments, the pleas and the menaces they addressed to the Pope.

So convinced were the King, the Cardinal, Norfolk and Anne that Clement had not made the base proposal attributed to him by Casali, so worried were they at the knowledge that he was not their puppet, that their first step was an attempt to use a bludgeon to force him to his knees. We say this because we read in Herbert's pages that :

" Gardiner and Fox, receiving their instructions in February, 1528, repair'd first to Francis, from whom they readily obtain'd a promise to cooperate puissantly with the Pope for effectuating the King's desire, as also a perswasory and menacing Letter in case of refusall to the Pope."[1]

Clement was virtually a prisoner at Orvieto when France and England conspired in this manner to threaten him with vengeance should he fail to do what Henry wanted. His jailer was Charles V of

[1] Herbert, *op. cit.*, p. 219.

Spain. He was menaced in this way with being crushed between the upper and nether millstone of the rivalry between the Western Powers at a time when, as we have pointed out in preceding chapters, Germany, Bohemia and Scandinavia were honeycombed with Lutheranism, when the Schismatic Church and Islam divided the East between them, when Muhammadanism appeared about to extend its pall to Italy and when that heroic company of matchless disputants, the Jesuits, had not yet sprung into being to lead a losing cause to new victories.

Clement's situation was made doubly perilous by the philosophy of that century as exemplified by the policies of Luther who conceded to the State a power by which matters of worship and doctrine were surrendered to the prince and civil authorities. From this conception of society it logically flowed that the pernicious doctrine " *cujus regio illius religio*," then held sway in many parts of the world.

It is not within our province to inquire whether Clement approved or censured this rule which sought to make it legal for the constituted authorities of the State to say what a man should or not believe. All that concerns our theme is that he was compelled to accept this point of view as a factor with which he had to deal. Sovereigns cannot brush aside living realities.

They told the Pope that if Henry, for personal reasons, and Francis on account of higher politics, were to break with the Church of Rome, their defection, under stress of this principle of " *cujus regio illius religio*," would immediately affect the freedom of worship of millions of Englishmen and Frenchmen. He was constrained to bear in mind what the decision of these two Kings would mean to men and women who took their faith most seriously and who were not smitten by the charms of a young woman thrust forward by designing politicians or moved by considerations of international comity. He had grave responsibilities to face, not that he necessarily cared who paid him homage but because the repercussion of his decision would be felt in every hamlet in England and France.

These considerations were not lost upon Fox or Gardiner as they pressed on to Orvieto. They had been chosen to carry out what Knight and Casali had been unable to accomplish because the former, the King's Almoner, was considered one of the best divines and the latter, the Cardinal's Chief Secretary, was the foremost canonist in England.[1] Gardiner was the abler of the two men and it was to him that Henry referred when he wrote to Anne :

" The bearer and his fellow are dispatched with as many things to compass our matter, and bring it to pass, as wit could imagine, which being accomplished by their diligence, I trust you and I will shortly have our desired end."[2]

If the King in this letter told her, whom he addressed as " mine own sweetheart," the real

---

[1] Burnet, *op. cit.*, Vol. I, p. 81.
[2] Brewer, *op. cit.*, Vol. II, p. 245.

reason why Gardiner and Fox were " dispatched with
as many things to compass our matter, and bring
it to pass, as wit could imagine," the Cardinal's
official instructions to them were to impress upon
the Holy See that :

"as Wolsey finds that the Pope has been labouring
under some misapprehension, as if the King had
set on foot this cause, not from fear of his succession,
but out of a vain affection or undue love to a gentlewoman of not so excellent qualities as she is here
esteemed, the Ambassadors are to assure the Pope
that the Cardinal would not, for any earthly affection
to his prince or desire of reward, transgress the
truth or swerve from the right path ; nor would he
have consented in any way to have reported to his
Holiness otherwise than his conviction of the
insufficiency of the marriage, nor have been guilty
of any dissimulation."[1]

So anxious was Wolsey to drive home the point
which we have so repeatedly stressed in these pages
that Henry " intended nothing more by these
proceedings than an examination into the legal
validity of his marriage, with the view, if possible
of removing all defects, and obviating any further
objections to Mary's legitimacy," that these instructions to Fox and Gardiner go on to affirm that:

" Wolsey is well assured, and dare put his soul,
that the King's desire is founded upon justice and
does not spring from any grudge or displeasure to
the Queen, whom the King loves and honours. . . .

---

[1] Brewer, *op. cit.*, Vol. II, p. 246.

But as this matrimony is contrary to God's law, the King's conscience is grievously offended."

Not content with making these assertions, and giving them an official character, in the very teeth of what Henry had written to Anne about " our matter," Wolsey, in these same instructions, spoke of the King's " own sweetheart " in these terms :

" On the other side, the approved excellent virtuous qualities of the said gentlewoman, the purity of her life, her constant virginity, her maidenly and woman pudicity, her soberness, chasteness, meekness, humility, wisdom, descent right noble and high through regal blood, . . . apparent aptness to procreation of children . . . be the grounds on which the King's desire is founded, which Wolsey regards as honest and necessary."[1]

It is not denied that during Anne's occasional absence from Court the letters Henry addressed to her " were conceived in a style of gross familiarity by no means calculated to inspire a favourable opinion of the ' pudicity ' of the writer or the receiver of them."[2] It was, nevertheless, so obviously in the interest of Norfolk and Suffolk and the anti-Wolsey faction to capitalize her charms and to use her as a Lorelei to draw the King into their net, that we do not say that the Cardinal was mistaken when he spoke of her " constant virginity." It is not improbable that precautions were taken by her political sponsors to assure Henry's subserviency

---

[1] Brewer, *op. cit.*, Vol. II, p. 246.
[2] *Ibid.*, p. 253.

to them by inciting his desire to possess her and by seeing, just in the nick of time, that he was frustrated. All that concerns our theme is that the record, as made up for Clement, eliminates Anne's personality and reveals Fox and Gardiner as insisting that Henry " intended nothing more by these proceedings than an examination into the legal validity of his marriage."

The Pope, from whom " the Defender of the Faith " and a Prince of his Church were thus concealing the truth, was found by Fox and Gardiner " lodged (at Orvieto) in an old ruinous Monastery, his outward chamber altogether unfurnished and his Bedchamber-hangings, together with his Bed, valued by them (as the Originall Letter hath it) at no more then twenty Nobles."[1] In these inhospitable surroundings Clement was confined to bed with swollen feet. There were suspicions that poison had been given him by the Imperialists, but Pastor assures us that the mischief was caused by his unwonted exertions on horseback on the night of his flight from Sant' Angelo.[2]

Although emaciated and in the most sorrowful frame of mind, [3] " the Pope yet receiv'd them (Fox and Gardiner) lovingly ; though not without the anxiety of one who could neither safely grant, nor deny the request of a King to whom he so much owed whatsoever liberty he enjoyed."[4]

---

[1] Herbert, *op. cit.*, p. 220.
[2] Pastor, *op. cit.*, Vol. X, p. 2.
[3] *Ibid.*, p. 1.
[4] Herbert, *op. cit.*, p. 220.

Both Henry and Wolsey knew of the sorry plight of the Pontiff to whom these emissaries were accredited. Clement had written them on December 14th, 1527, autograph letters which spoke of "ignominious punishment," "daily danger to our lives," "misery in Rome," and "personal sufferings."[1] We cannot blame Fox and Gardiner for going ahead with their mission when they found the Pope in so abject a state. It was their duty to their Master to take full advantage of conditions known to their principals, and to them, when they accepted their mandate.

The threatening letter from Francis of France was not presented at the very first audience. The distinguished divine and the skilled canonist were far too astute to begin negotiations in such an impolitic manner. On the contrary, they submitted to Clement a thesis or book which Henry had prepared containing a theological dissertation in favour of the argument which they were instructed to press upon the Holy See.[2]

Sitting upon a bench hidden by a coverlet worth but a few pence, the Pope read the opening chapter and the latter part of the treatise. Commenting upon it, as he turned the leaves, he said that he would keep it and study it at his leisure.

Before dismissing Fox and Gardiner he asked them whether the King had ever broken the matter to the Queen. They replied in the affirmative, adding that

[1] Pastor, *op. cit.*, Vol. X, p. 7.
[2] Brewer, *op. cit.*, Vol. II, p. 250.

she was content to abide by the judgment of the
Church. The Pope then inquired, in a more or less
casual manner, whether there was any truth in the
rumour that Wolsey was opposed to the annulment
of the marriage. Gardiner, not suspecting the drift
of the question, eagerly testified to the Cardinal's
zeal in its favour. Clement calmly retorted that,
in such a case, he could not be accepted as an
impartial judge.[1] This brought the first audience
to a close.

Gardiner, for he completely overshadowed his
colleague, had been charged to obtain a Bull for
Wolsey in conjunction with a Roman Cardinal,
directing them to try the case, and, if they should be
satisfied of certain facts, which it was assumed were
readily demonstrable, to declare the marriage null
and void. The Pope's question showed that even
though his privy chamber was " all naked and
unhanged, the roofs fallen down "[2] his sense of
responsibility was acute and that he placed no trust
in Wolsey's impartiality. We thus find that this
first audience of the King's third diplomatic mission
to the Papacy demonstrates that Clement's attention
was riveted upon the necessity of curtailing Wolsey's
judicial attributes.

Gardiner's tactics were directed toward over-
coming this objection. The more he urged that
a Papal Commission should be issued giving Plenary
authority to the Cardinal the more insistently was

[1] *Quarterly Review*, January, 1877, *op. cit.*, p. 30.
[2] Brewer, *op. cit.*, Vol. II, p. 249.

the reply made that it would be better if Wolsey " meddled not as a judge in this matter."[1]

The King's Ambassador finally lost patience, and, raising his voice, found inspiration in Francis's letter and in the Pope's abject misery. But the more Gardiner fumed the calmer became Clement who, seeing how imperative it was that he should not lose his patience, quietly observed that he was not learned—the more the pity. He must be ruled, he observed, by his lawyers and they could not, or at all events would not, give their sanction to Gardiner's demands.

This remark caused the Englishman to grow sarcastic and to exclaim in Latin " *Quod Pontifex habet omnia jura in scrinio pectoris* "—the Pope had all laws locked up in the cabinet of his breast. Clement, in no sense baffled by this retort, at once replied : " This is true, my son, but I must confess that God has never given me the key with which to open it."

" Who could fail," asks Brewer, " to appreciate the temper of a Pope who could take refuge, after four hours of incessant badgering, in a witticism conceived at his own expense ? Able disputant as Gardiner was, and there were few abler, the imperturbable good humour of Clement was more than a match for all his energy and his eloquence."[2]

This episode, to our mind, is worth a volume of commentary. It defines Clement's character. It

---

[1] Brewer, *op. cit.*, Vol. II, p. 251.
[2] *Ibid.*, p. 252.

shows that if he was not of a robust temperament, he was of a conciliatory disposition, keenly conscious of his responsibilities and alive to the fact that in his helpless condition he could not afford to jeopardize the spiritual heritage of millions of his children by fulminating against the recalcitrant Ambassador.

The fact that he stood up against " four hours of incessant badgering " and not only kept his patience but adhered to his position demonstrates that Froude and other detractors do him grave injustice when they attribute his conduct to fear of Charles V. Had such an ignoble motive guided him, fear might have forced him to maintain his ground, but it would not have engendered that serenity of soul that remained unruffled under such trying conditions. Cowards cringe and cringing often hold fast to whatever loophole there may be available to them, but it takes a clear conscience and a stout heart to remain serene and adamant in gloomy surroundings and in the face of a volcanic torrent of abuse and menace.

A man who spoke Latin as fluently as Gardiner was a trained disputant. A few days later he returned to the charge and submitted an alternative proposition in the shape of a general commission but in terms less stringent than those that had been devised in England. He had repeatedly been urged by Clement's advisers to propose another draft. " We were always told," he wrote, " that it should be of our own devising. But when it was drawn and

submitted to them, every one had some fault to find.
. . . They praised the present flavour of the meat
but blamed the cooking."[1] It was finally agreed that
Cardinal Campeggio should go to England and
" with the Cardinal of York (Wolsey) try the validity
of the King's marriage."[2]

This means that the Pope, while not depriving
Wolsey of his Legatine authority, subordinated him
to Campeggio and made of the Italian Cardinal the
pivotal factor in the case and of the English prelate
what is technically known as an " assessor." This
important distinction appears to have escaped even
so brilliant a writer as Brewer. He seems to
attribute Campeggio's prominence, in the subsequent trial, not to what was " nominated in the
bond," but to his more intimate acquaintance with
the Canon Law of procedure.[3] We stress the point
that his dominant position grew out of the very
nature of his functions.

Men trained in the Common Law of England, or
who are part and parcel of the civilization of which
it is the expression, are prone to misunderstand the
radical difference between the effective power of a
" presiding judge " and that of an " assessor."
The line of cleavage is far greater than is revealed
by a mere examination of printed texts. It is in the

[1] Brewer, *op. cit.*, Vol. II, p. 252.

[2] Burnet, Vol. I, p. 84. See also Burnet, Vol. II, p. 55.

[3] Let us quote Brewer's exact words : " His (Campeggio's) superior
knowledge of the practice of the Roman Courts gave him considerable
advantage. Thus Wolsey fell, from the very first, into the position of
an inferior judge or assessor." (Vol. I, p. 292.) See also Burnet, *op.
cit.*, Vol. I, p. 121, and more particularly note for evidence of Campeggio's primacy over Wolsey.

warp of the fabric but it is not revealed to the eye.
We fear that it is because this differentiation has
escaped them that those who have discussed Henry's
divorce have apparently not seen how radically the
orientation of the entire scene changed when Wolsey
was relegated to a subordinate part in the tragedy.

As long as Gardiner sought to make of the Cardinal
the central figure of the Legatine Court, Lorenzo
Pucci was most reluctant to granting him a
Commission. Every word of it was not only weighed
but put under a magnifying glass. When, however,
it was agreed that Campeggio should take the lead
or, as Burnet expresses it, that " he with the Cardinal
of York, might try the validity of the King's
marriage," the matter assumed a new aspect, and
what had appeared to be an insurmountable difficulty
quickly disappeared. The Pope trusted Campeggio.
He refrained from endangering the religious freedom
of English burghers and French peasants by
challenging Henry and Francis as soon as Wolsey
accepted to have his judicial attributes thus effectively
curtailed.

Gardiner was not entirely satisfied with the
Commission he had obtained. It did not declare
that the decision of the Legatine Court would be
final and it did not say that no appeal would lie
from it to Rome. " He was," says Brewer, " outwitted, notwithstanding his quickness, ability and
decision."[1]

Our great admiration for the scholarship of the

---

[1] Brewer, *op. cit.*, Vol. II, p. 253.

author of the *Reign of Henry VIII* does not prevent us from dissenting from this deduction. Gardiner was a partisan endeavouring to further his Master's interests. Clement had other duties and responsibilities. If he imposed his will upon the English Ambassador, it was not that he had " outwitted " him but that he refused to yield to falsehoods, blandishments and threats.

CHAPTER IX

THE DECRETAL BULL

GARDINER was far too able a canonist not to have caught the distinction between a Legatine Court presided over by Wolsey and one upon which the Cardinal was " an inferior judge or assessor."[1] The latter was also much too astute not to have seen this difference. But the King, with all his knowledge of theology and his training as a dialectician, knew nothing of the adjective law of the Church. His acquaintance with Canon Law was confined to what is technically known as substantive law. And Norfolk and Suffolk, and of course Anne, understood nothing about such matters.

Gardiner and Wolsey had interests at stake that precluded the possibility of their apprising Henry and their political enemies of the fly in the ointment. The canonists of the realm were either not aware of the details of what was going on or they were too closely allied to the Wolsey faction to raise their voices. The net result of all this was that the Ambassador and the Cardinal held their tongue and Henry, Norfolk, Suffolk and Anne did not have their peace of mind unduly disturbed.

It was because Gardiner had realized that he

---

[1] Brewer, *op. cit.*, Vol. II, p. 292.

could neither deceive, cajole nor intimidate Clement
into granting the Commission desired by Wolsey
that he accepted what was offered him. He saw
that it was that or nothing. He knew that if he
came home empty handed his hopes of advancement
would be blighted. He, therefore, decided to make
the best of a bad bargain, confident that as he had
the Cardinal's ear, Wolsey would defend him. And
he counted upon Fox presenting the matter to the
King in the best possible light.

The messenger upon whom Gardiner depended
was so diplomatic in his explanations of what had
taken place at Orvieto, so adroit in imputing to the
Pope a verbal promise that the sentence of the
Legatine Court would be confirmed that the King
took these observations " marvellously thankfully
and made marvellous demonstrations of joy and
gladness, calling in Mistress Anne and causing
(Fox) to repeat the same thing again before her."[1]
It was because the wish is so often father to the
thought and because Henry had failed to see that
the Commission granted by Clement implied the
subordination of Wolsey to Campeggio that he
received this report with such " marvellous demonstrations of joy and gladness."

The Cardinal, knowing that Gardiner had
failed and recognizing that this failure, following
upon what had happened to Knight and Casali,
meant that the Pope would not lend his high office
to the creation of a species of Wolsey drum-head

[1] Brewer, *op. cit.*, Vol. II, p. 254.

court-martial, accepted the inevitable and concentrated his attention upon doing the best he could with the means available to him. We have just seen that Fox had reported that a verbal promise had been obtained from the Pope to the effect that he would confirm the sentence and never revoke the case. Wolsey laid great stress upon this alleged assurance. He kept the mind of the King fixed upon it, insisting that if it were put in writing, in the form of what is technically known as a " Decretal Bull," all would be well.

Let us endeavour to understand what the Cardinal thus had in view. The subject is somewhat technical and we are by no means certain that we can make it as clear as we should like. We shall, however, be taking a step in the right direction if we begin by bearing in mind that Henry's " scrupulosity of conscience " provoked both a question of fact and several questions of law.

The question of fact may be thus resumed :

(1) Did Arthur and Catherine consummate their marriage ?

The questions of law may be reduced to four, which we thus summarize :

(1) When Leviticus (XVIII,16) decrees " thou shalt not uncover the nakedness of thy brother's wife ; it *is* thy brother's nakedness," does it ordain an absolute inhibition *jure divino* or does it merely prescribe a general rule admitting of exceptions in the form of a Papal dispensation ?

I

(2) When Deuteronomy (XXV, 5) declares that " if brethren dwell together, and one of them die, and have no child, the wife of the dead shall not marry without unto a stranger : her husband's brother shall go in unto her, and take her to him to wife, and perform the duty of an husband's brother unto her," does it formulate a principle which in any way modifies Leviticus XVIII, 16 ?

(3) Does this Levitical text apply to all marriages duly celebrated, whether consummated or not, or does it take effect solely in the case of those which have been consummated, and

(4) Were the terms of the Dispensation granted by Julius II applicable to a consummated marriage or were they restricted to one that had not been consummated ?

Wolsey felt absolutely certain that he could demonstrate that Arthur and Catherine had consummated their union. We have already seen that he had advised Henry that it made no difference whether they had or not, because they had been married, as he put it, in *facie ecclesiæ*. This sufficed, he said, to make the Levitical inhibition applicable to the marriage between Henry and Catherine. But the Cardinal was far too practical a man to think of predicating the King's case upon an abstract question of law when he felt certain that it could be won upon the facts.

Wolsey knew that he could count not only upon the collaboration of the Norfolk faction but also upon the testimony of such influential persons as the dowager Duchess of Norfolk, George Earl of Shrewsbury, Robert Viscount Fitz-water and Thomas Duke of Norfolk. He was assured that they would testify that Arthur had had carnal knowledge of Catherine.

In placing upon his political adversaries the onus of establishing Henry's contention the Cardinal prepared a pitfall for them should their evidence fail to convince Campeggio. He took sardonic pleasure in contemplating that he could use Agnes " the old *Duchesse* of Norfolke," to attempt to rebut the statement made by Sanders that " a grave matron " had been " put into the same bed with him (Arthur) to hinder the prince from knowing her (Catherine) Carnally."[1] And it probably gratified his baser instincts to be able to force " Thomas Duke of Norfolke, Lord Treasurer of England " to depose that :

" he being the day of the Marriage in the Bishop of London's Palace, and the morrow after, at the Prince's Breakfast, heard the Prince's words to Maurice St. John, when he said hee had been that night in the midst of *Spain*; by which words, as also because Prince *Arthur* was a Gentleman of good Complexion and nature, and above fifteen, he beleeves that he carnally knew his Lady, because himself at the same age did carnally know and use ; and that he beleeves this the rather, that he heard from Credible persons that the said Prince *Arthur* did lie with the said Ladie Catherine five or six nights afterwards."[2]

[1] Herbert, *op. cit.*, p. 242.
[2] *Ibid.*, p. 244.

Having at his disposal the entire administrative machinery of the State to search every nook and corner of England to locate whatever witnesses he might require, Wolsey welcomed the opportunity of having the King's case turn upon a question of fact.   He felt that if he could obtain in advance a " Decretal Bull " disposing of the controverted legal niceties involved, success would be assured whoever presided at the trial.   It made no difference to him how much Campeggio might overshadow him provided the Pope agreed to invalidate the marriage in the event of it being proved that Arthur and Catherine had consummated their union.

It was for these reasons that, when Gardiner's report reached him, Wolsey determined to insist that before the Court began to hear witnesses a written ruling should be made by the Pope to the effect that the inhibition contained in Leviticus was part of the divine law, admitting of no exception or dispensation,[1] although applicable solely to consummated marriages.   Such a definition of canon law is what is technically known as a " Decretal Bull." The Cardinal's purpose was not to have Clement pass upon the extent of the relations between Arthur and Catherine but merely to have a preliminary ruling from the Holy See that in the event of their having consummated their marriage, the Dispensation granted to Henry and Catherine was invalid.

We   know   that   on   Gardiner's   insistence   a

[1] Lingard, *op. cit.*, Vol. IV, p. 503.

" Decretal Bull " was issued by Clement. Unfortunately, we cannot quote its exact provisions for the very simple reason that no trace of it exists. It was entrusted to Campeggio who was instructed to show it to Henry, not to allow him to copy it and to destroy it as soon as the King had read it. These facts are thus set forth by Henry himself in a published statement of his case :

" On his first scruple the King sent to the Bishop of Rome, as Christ's Vicar, who had the key of knowledge to dissolve his doubts. The said Bishop . . . delegated his whole powers to Campeggio and Wolsey, giving them also a special commission in the form of a Decretal, wherein he declared the King's marriage null and empowered him to marry again. In the open commission also he gave them full authority to give sentence for the King. Secretly he gave them instructions to burn the Commission Decretal and not proceed upon it ; (but) at the time of sending the commission he also sent the King a brief, written in his own hand, admitting the justice of his cause and promising *sanctissime sub verbo Pontificis* that he would never advocate it to Rome."[1]

Froude asserts that this " Decretal Bull," which he had not seen any more than we have, " pre-judged the case."[2] He goes on to say that the Pope " had anticipated judgment though he dared not avow it."[3] And he sums up the matter by adding that " the

---

[1] Froude, *op. cit.*, p. 67.
[2] *Ibid.*, p. 75.
[3] *Ibid.*, p. 95.

secret Decretal had ruled what the decision was to be."[1] We prefer to be less emphatic as we are groping in the dark. It seems to be possible that the purview of the " Decretal Bull " was misinterpreted by Gardiner and misunderstood by Henry— and that Froude has misconstrued it.

We are not even sure that Gardiner saw it before it was entrusted to Campeggio. If he did, he could not have afforded to be overtechnical about its terms. We have already set forth the reasons which lead us to this deduction—how he knew that he could neither deceive, flatter nor coerce the Pope into giving the King an unfair advantage over the Queen, that the Cardinal desired a preliminary ruling upon a point of law and that he had to take what he had been offered or admit that he had failed to carry out the orders given him. A man of his temperament who had his back against the wall and who may have seen visions of his own head on a block would certainly have been tempted to misinterpret in his favour the tenor of a document which he knew that nobody would be permitted to scrutinize.

It was the simplest thing in the world for Henry to have misunderstood the letter which he says that Clement wrote " admitting the justice of his cause." But the King forgot, when he issued this published statement, that " his cause," as he explained it to the Pope, was not the annulment of his marriage with Catherine but his professed desire to have his conscience put at ease. He had remarked, even

---

[1] Froude, *op. cit.*, p. 95.

after receiving this letter, that " he wanted nothing more than a declaration whether this marriage was valid or not."[1]   Hall, a contemporary writer, makes him say, at about this same time, that if the Queen were adjudged by the law of God as his lawful wife,

" there was never thing more pleasant nor more acceptable to me in my life, both for the discharge and clearing of my conscience, and also for the good qualities and conditions which I know to be in her. For I assure you all, that beside her noble parentage, of the which she is descended, she is a woman of most gentleness, of most humility and buxomness ; yea of all good qualities appertaining to nobility she is without comparison, as I this twenty years almost have had the true experiment, or that if I were to marry again, if the marriage might be good, I would surely choose her above all women."[2]

It is the duty of the Holy See to be well-informed about what is going on in the world.   There are always wheels within wheels and it behoves the Papacy to understand the significance of every major event that takes place in every capital.   It is encumbent upon the Pope to have the leading men of every country duly card-indexed ~~in his mind~~. We may assume, therefore, that Clement knew all about Henry's marital infidelities, Wolsey's insatiable ambition, the jealousy of Norfolk and Suffolk and of the English aristocracy, their desire to overthrow the Cardinal, the orientation of English foreign

---

[1] Brewer, *op. cit.*, Vol. II, p. 298.
[2] *Ibid.*, p. 307.

policy towards France and against Spain, the interpretation placed by the King on the fact that he had
no surviving male issue, Wolsey's attempt to make
use of this superstition in order to have Catherine
cast off and her place taken by a French princess,
and the bold move of the leaders of the Norfolk
faction to outwit the Cardinal and to gain power for
themselves by capitalizing the charms of Anne
Boleyn and by making a magnet out of her " constant
virginity."

The Pope, with these facts before him, was able to
view the King's conduct in its proper perspective.
He saw a man torn by two conflicting emotions, a
religious background beset by sensuality, a patriot
consumed by lust, a sovereign who was morally
weak turned into a puppet by designing politicians,
one set pulling to the right and the other to the
left, but both desiring to get rid of Catherine for
equally inadmissible reasons.

Clement sympathized with Henry's mental
anguish. He sought to assuage it. He construed
the King's appeals to the Holy See as being those
of a Catholic whose dominant motives were
honourable and who was entitled to find solace in
the bosom of his Church. The door of hope is
never closed to a penitent, whatever his life may be.
It strikes us that the spiritual consolation for which
Henry said that he strove was something to which
he was legitimately entitled.

All that he asked for, in addressing the Pope, was
that his conscience be set at ease by a judgment of a

duly constituted ecclesiastical Tribunal.   Clement
in sending " the King a brief written in his own hand,
admitting the justice of his (the King's) cause "—
we have just repeated Henry's exact words—
referred not to the merits of the controversy upon
which this ecclesiastical Court should rule but to
the King's right to be heard.

It is regrettable that the facts about the " Decretal
Bull " cannot be gone into with the same explicitness.
All we can say is that Froude's deduction and that
of other authors are based upon insufficient evidence.

It is with surprise that we read in that most
Catholic of works, Pastor's *History of the Popes*, that :

" The contents of this document (the Decretal
Bull) can only be conjectured, but it must have been
of such a character as to have made the divorce
between Henry and Catherine possible and even an
accomplished fact, had not the Pope entirely withheld
it from the free disposal of Henry and Wolsey.   Even
if Clement, in granting this illusory document, which
confirmed the demands of Henry to their full extent,
was guilty of incredible weakness, yet he was acting
under the belief that the grievous blunder thus
committed could be repaired by depriving the Bull of
any practical use . . . by declaring firmly and
clearly that he could never have allowed it to be put
into execution."[1]

It is an extremely hazardous thing for an historian
to pronounce so far reaching a decision when he is
constrained to admit that the " contents of this

---

[1] Pastor, *op. cit.*, Vol. X, p. 261.

document can only be conjectured." The brilliant author whom we are now putting on the grill is described as " Professor of History in the University of Innsbruck and Director of the Austrian Historical Institute in Rome." He has looked at his data from the point of view of a student and not from that of a barrister. Had he been learned in the law, he would not have been so dogmatic.

Lingard, as we have already seen, says that the " Decretal Bull " which Gardiner sought to obtain from Clement was a ruling by " which the Pope was made to pronounce in favour of the prohibition in Leviticus and to declare that it was part of the divine law admitting of no exception or Dispensation."[1] The proof that Clement refused to make any such pronouncement is brought out by the fact that the Legatine Court admitted evidence in regard to the intimate marital relations between Arthur and Catherine. Had Clement issued the " Decretal Bull " that Gardiner had submitted for his signature, no such testimony would have been necessary.

Such a decision would have eliminated the need of adducing evidence to prove that Arthur had had carnal knowledge of Catherine. It would for all practical purposes have ended the case. The conclusion is thus forced upon us that the " Decretal Bull," as signed by the Pope, passed judgment simply and solely upon a question of law and did not impinge upon the facts of the case. It decided

[1] Lingard, *op. cit.*, Vol. IV, p. 503.

that the text of the Dispensation invoked[1] by Henry was so worded that it was inoperative if Arthur and Catherine had consummated their union. It left that issue, one not of law but of fact, to the Legatine Court.

Of course, all we are doing in making these statements is to oppose our conjecture to that of other authors. Their hypotheses, however, are faced with the fact that the King himself offered parole evidence to prove that Arthur and Catherine had consummated their marriage, testimony that would have been entirely unnecessary if the Pope had issued a " Decretal Bull " in the sense defined by Froude and Pastor.

We, therefore, have no hesitation in arraying our opinion against the hard and fast verdict of Pastor the Catholic and Froude the Protestant. Had either of them looked at the matter from the stand-point of a lawyer he would have seen that instead of allowing the Legatine Court to rule upon the point of law involved, Clement did so himself. He converted Campeggio and Wolsey into a jury of two charged to submit the facts to the law as defined by him. Such an attitude, if understood in its true light, merits neither the aspersions of Pastor nor the calumny of Froude.

---

[1] We say " invoked " by Henry because his contention then was that he desired that his marriage should be validated.

CHAPTER X

CAMPEGGIO

CARDINAL LORENZO CAMPEGGIO, who for the next five chapters will play a prominent part in our narrative, was an eminent canonist and experienced statesman. He had taken holy orders after the death of his wife in 1509, and the red hat was conferred upon him in 1517. He had repeatedly been employed by Popes Leo X and Adrian VI in delicate and important negotiations.[1] The diplomatic world regarded him as a friend of Catherine's nephew, Charles V. Francis I did not take kindly to him; but Henry liked him, had named him to the Bishopric of Salisbury and had lately made him a present of a palace in Rome.

It was Gardiner, or, according to Herbert, the King himself, who had suggested that the Commission "to Heare and Determine the Cause in *England*," should be granted to Wolsey and Campeggio.[2] Clement welcomed the proposal to select the latter because it enabled him to entrust a most delicate mission to a prelate of outstanding ability who was recommended by Henry and who enjoyed Charles's friendship and respect.

[1] Lingard, Vol. IV, p. 508.
[2] Herbert, *op. cit.*, p. 220.

Campeggio did his utmost to decline the appointment because he was a martyr to gout. The English Ambassador was, however, importunate and the Pope saw in the infirmity of the Legate an additional reason for selecting him.

Froude speaks of Campeggio's dilatoriness[1] and of his " loitering on his way, as he had been directed, pretending difficulties of the road."[2] Herbert tells us that " the pace of *Campegius* (the promised Legat) also appear'd staggering and slow, and all that might frustrate the King's intentions was secretly practiced."[3] Burnet is more explicit. He records that " the Cardinal (Campeggio) made great excuses ; he was then Legate at Rome, in which he had such advantages that he had no mind to enter a business which must forever engage either the Emperor or the King against him. He also pretended an inability to travel so great a journey, being much subject to the gout."[4]

The hardships of travel were so great in those days, that we can well understand that Campeggio took his time in getting from Orvieto to London. It is quite probable that his arrival was delayed, as Brewer expresses it, " by real or diplomatic fits of the gout, perhaps by both."[5] There was, nevertheless, another factor which this distinguished historian appears to have overlooked.

The Commission empowering the two Cardinals,

---

[1] Froude, *op. cit.*, p. 84.
[2] *Ibid.*, p. 74.
[3] Herbert, *op. cit.*, p. 223.
[4] Burnet, *op. cit.*, Vol. II, p. 84.
[5] Brewer, *op. cit.*, Vol. II, p. 290.

Campeggio and Wolsey, to " Heare and Determine the Cause in England " was dated, Viterbo, July 23rd, 1528.[1]   In May, 1528, the sweating sickness made its terrible appearance in England with greater severity than before.   This time its ravages extended to the Court and the upper classes and the brevity of its attacks was more than offset by their violence.[2]

We cannot blame a man advanced in years and full of honours, who unquestionably was " sore vexed with the gout,"[3] and who did his utmost to refuse a disagreeable mission pregnant with all kinds of unpleasant complications, if he showed great reluctance to rush into a country stricken by an epidemic of disease.   The human equation should never be overlooked in analysing problems of State. It is the duty of a Cardinal to confront pestilence and hardships in order to bring spiritual consolation to the afflicted.   But it is not encumbent upon a prelate to dash headlong into a pesthole to execute a mission such as that which called Campeggio to England.

Reasons of practical common sense, which had nothing to do with his gout or with any conception of self-preservation, may well have prompted him in delaying his departure and in tarrying on the road. While we have emphasized the fact that Henry's official reason for bringing Campeggio to London had nothing to do with a passionate longing to

---

[1] Herbert, *op. cit.*, p. 220.
[2] Brewer, *op. cit.*, Vol. II, p. 271, and Strickland, *op. cit.*, Vol. II, p. 539.
[3] Cavendish, *op. cit.*, p. 209.

possess Anne Boleyn, everybody interested in the case knew, in the spring of 1528, that lust as much as " scrupulosity of conscience " moved the King in pressing for a judicial decision concerning the legality of his marriage. It meant a great deal to Clement and Campeggio to learn that this sweating sickness had so completely flabbergasted Henry that he " had sent Anne home to her friends, returned to the company and conversation of Catherine and shared in her devotional exercises."[1]

We know that Henry was very superstitious. His conduct in thus participating in the Queen's prayers may be explained by the fact that " on Tuesday the 16th of June (1528), Anne Boleyn ' one of the ladies of the Chamber ' caught the infection."[2] He felt that such a visitation from heaven required not only that she should be returned to her father's house at Hever but that " he should make his will and take the sacraments, for fear of sudden death."[3]

Another author tells us that when the pestilence was raging " the King made thirty-nine wills and confessed his sins every day."[4] A letter written by the Bishop of Lincoln, dated June 28th, 1528, conveys the information that :

" this day (Sunday, 28 June) he hath received the good Lord, and so has the more part that be about him, and he rejoices much that he has done so, and says he is armed towards God and the world."[5]

---

[1] Strickland, Vol. II, p. 539.
[2] Brewer, *op. cit.*, Vol. II, p. 273.
[3] *Ibid.*, p. 273.
[4] Strickland, *op. cit.*, Vol. II, p. 539.
[5] Brewer, *op. cit.*, Vol. II, p. 274 (note).

It is obvious, therefore, that when both Froude and Brewer speak of Campeggio's dilatoriness, and when other writers assume that his slow progress was prompted by ignoble motives and a desire on the part of the Pope to carry water on both shoulders, they overlook the factors of which we have just spoken.

It is admitted that " prudence is the better part of valour," and that " fools rush in where wise men fear to tread."   Our contention is that in the summer of 1528, it behoved Campeggio to keep out of England, and to let the evolution of Henry's " scrupulosity of conscience," which was then in a new phase, develop normally. Had the Italian Legate then come to the English Court, with the pomp and pageantry called for by his exalted mission, his lack of tact would have been unpardonable.

This argument can be carried still further.   We would approve the Pope's tactics even if it were demonstrated that there had been intentional dilatoriness, occasioned neither by the then fluid state of Henry's mentality nor by fear of the epidemic of sweating sickness.   We are endeavouring to ascertain Clement's point of view.   It was that of the head of the Catholic Church whose duty it was to think of his responsibility to his Maker.   If we desire to be fair to him we cannot eliminate this element from our consideration.

Clement could not close his eyes to the fact that this judicial inquiry into the validity of Catherine's marriage—whether its genuine objective was to cast her aside or merely to remove any defects latent in her union with Henry and obviate any future objections to Mary's legitimacy—was bound to be resented by her nephew, the Emperor. From the standpoint of the interests of Catholicism, there was nothing to be gained and everything to be risked in convoking this Legatine Court. It behoved the Pope, as the responsible executive of the Catholic Church, to bear this in mind.

Starting from the premiss of there being everything to lose and nothing to gain for Catholicism in the whole unfortunate business, the attention of Clement was directed to the fact that, were circumstances again to create a community of interests between England and Spain, as they had quite recently, nothing could be more desirable than the maintenance of this marriage. He understood foreign politics. He knew that Wolsey was an English patriot who was opposed to Charles partly because the growing influence of the Emperor disturbed the European balance of power.[1] But the Pope saw that this equilibrium would be changed overnight should Francis succeed in the policy then pursued by the House of Valois of courting the friendship of Sulyman the Magnificent.[2]

Wolsey had fanned Henry's conscientious scruples because of pro-French leanings.[3] Clement thought of the future and doubted the permanence of this

---

[1] Robertson, *op. cit.*, Vol. II, p. 274, and Froude, *op. cit.*, p. 26.
[2] The Ottoman " Capitulations " granted to Francis I in 1535 gave France a preponderating position in the Near East.
[3] Brewer, Vol. II, p. 267.

K

orientation of higher politics. It was extremely unpopular in England.[1] The labouring classes, suffering from unemployment and bad harvests, were opposed to the Cardinal, and the Norfolk faction hated him.[2]   All these facts were fully known to the Pope. He thus felt that the government then in power at London was far from secure, that it menaced the cause of peace and that a change of Ministry would not only obviate war between England and Spain but enable Catherine to retain her crown and, perhaps, satisfy Norfolk and Suffolk by permitting their political pawn to rule as the King's favourite.

These deductions are obviously nothing but conjectures. We do not place undue stress upon them. We suggest, nevertheless, that the facts upon which they are based should be weighed in the scales before the Pope is charged with weakness and deceit because he believed in making haste slowly. Time has solved many problems for the Church of Rome. It is not consonant with the rules of fair play to charge a chief of State with having been guided by base motives when considerations of an ethical nature can readily be adduced to account for what he did.

Campeggio, " incessantly tormented with the gout,"[3] reached Paris in mid-September, 1528. He was to have been received on his entry into the French capital, by fifteen or sixteen bishops and

---

[1] Brewer, Vol. II, p. 267.
[2] *Ibid.*, p. 267.
[3] Brewer, *op. cit.*, Vol. II, p. 291

archbishops and " a right good company," but being desirous of avoiding ostentatious display, although scarcely able to sit on horseback, he hurried forward in order to avoid any such demonstration. During his audience with Francis he allowed it to be known that the Pope had instructed him to use his utmost endeavour to reconcile the King and the Queen and not to proceed to sentence until he had received a new Commission from Rome.[1]

Brewer, who gives the information which we have just reproduced, says that " it is scarcely probable that so cautious a diplomatist would have so imprudently betrayed himself." He adds :

" The intelligence, however obtained, was conveyed to Wolsey. It was a prelude to the troubles that awaited him and must have warned him that he would not find in Campeggio so docile or compliant a coadjutor in procuring the King's divorce as he had expected. In fact Campeggio assumed an authority superior to his own, and, without consulting his colleague, had determined on the course that should be adopted."[2]

We have the greatest respect for Brewer's scholarship and sense of justice. He was a divine of the English Church[3] but he has not written of Henry's divorce in a spirit of Protestant partisanship. We fear, however, that because he was not trained in Latin law he fell into the error brought out in the preceding paragraph.

---

[1] Brewer, *op. cit.*, Vol. II, p. 292.
[2] *Ibid.*, p. 292.
[3] *Quarterly Review* , January, 1877, *op. cit.* ,p. 48.

We have already explained that the very nature of Campeggio's functions made him the dominant factor in the Legatine Court and not merely Wolsey's coadjutor. A presiding judge of a Latin bench, whether it be a " *Chambre Civile du Tribunal de la Seine*," now sitting in Paris, or an ecclesiastical body, acts upon his own responsibility. He takes the bit in his teeth and, while studiously courteous to his associates, makes his personality felt. He is, and upon this we insist, not the coadjutor but the hierarchical superior of his assessors. *Il dirige les débats* is the French way of saying that the entire machinery of the Court is in his hands.

It is by no means improbable that Campeggio, who was fully conversant with the extent of his attributes, said that he would use his utmost endeavour to reconcile the King and Queen and that he gave out this information, upon his initiative and without consulting Wolsey. The meaning of this announcement may have escaped Brewer. He would not have referred to Campeggio as Wolsey's " coadjutor " if it had not. And he could not be expected to have known that it was Campeggio's duty to seek to reconcile Henry and Catherine. Trained in the Common Law of England, or rather living in an environment dominated by its beneficent rules, he failed to grasp the fact that Canon Law—like the modern French Civil Law[1]—makes it the duty of the trial judge to seek to restore harmony among warring spouses.

---

[1] French Civil Code, *Articles* 238 *et seq.*

To the mind of an Englishman a judge is a judge and not an official peace-maker. Canon Law and the modern French Civil Law look at the matter from another point of view. They ordain that in matters affecting the status of a married couple he shall first attempt to reconcile the parties before sitting in judgment upon their case.

It is obvious, then, that Campeggio was guilty of no indiscretion if he stated that he intended to strive to bring Henry and Catherine together, even if the matter that called him to England had assumed the technical form of an action where the sole official objective was to ease the King's conscience. We have been led to stress this point not because we attach any special importance to it but because it is a typical instance of the misunderstandings that shroud the subject which we are discussing.

The gout played havoc with Campeggio during his stay in Paris. He was " marvellously tormented " and uttered many a bitter *Kyrie eleyson* during the paroxysms of this importunate disease. When he reached Montreuil he was still carried in a litter, writes the English Ambassador to Paris who joined his suite, " his feet not being able to abide the sqwasse (pressure) of the stirrup or his hands to hold the bridle."[1] He arrived at London on October 7th, 1528, and lodged at the house of the Duke of Suffolk, that is to say at the home of one of Wolsey's outstanding critics and an ardent champion of Anne.

---

[1] Brewer, *op. cit.*, Vol. II, p. 296.

No explanation can be found for this choice of residence. We accordingly assume that those who were responsible for the arrangement for Campeggio's welfare made the selection. The sixteenth century, however, knew nothing of comfort, and it is therefore not surprising to learn that ten days later—he had been transported in the meantime to Bath House—he wrote that " I am still confined to my bed, my agony being greater than usual owing to my journey. I do not know when I shall be sufficiently free from pain to be able to visit the King."

Wolsey had too much at stake to allow Campeggio to get adequate rest. The King had long since forgotten about the sweating sickness and about " the true fit of compunction "[1] it had engendered. " Henry's penitence," writes one of Catherine's biographers, " was precisely of the same nature as that described in some oft-quoted lines relative to his sable Majesty ' when sick ' : the pest abated, the King's jovial spirits returned ; he wrote love-letters to his beautiful favourite and huffed his wife."[2]

Wolsey, knowing that Henry's passion was again aflame, dared not risk his ascendancy by giving the Italian Cardinal a moment's respite. He hastened to Bath House and insisted upon talking business. Campeggio was in excruciating agony but did not repel the assault, seeking, nevertheless, to begin

[1] Strickland, *op. cit.*, Vol. II, p. 539.
[2] *Ibid.*, p. 539.

at the beginning, that is to say to consider first and foremost the question of finding ways and means of effecting a reconciliation. We have already seen that this attitude was imposed upon him by Canon Law. It opened up a vista which was not agreeable to Wolsey who knew that Henry was straining at the leash and yearning to rush into Anne's arms.

Campeggio was too experienced a diplomatist to allow his coadjutor or assessor to dictate to him. He had a mission to carry out and he was determined to accomplish it according to the rules of the game. Wolsey was equally politic and equally determined. He felt that he, too, had a mandate to execute. He considered that he owed it to his King—and to his own safety—to do what Henry wanted and make Anne Queen of England within the least possible delay.

We can imagine these two Cardinals, one writhing upon a bed of pain, and exclaiming, from time to time, when the argument crowded him too closely, " *Kyrie eleyson*," and the other, in the full majesty of his robes of office, seeking to carry his point and to take advantage of this physical incapacity of his fellow-judge. These dramatic sidelights in this tragedy in the life of a Queen advancing in age and married to a King younger in years and bubbling over with sensuality are brought out in this report sent by Campeggio to the Holy See :

" As I am still confined to my bed his Lordship (Wolsey) came three or four times to visit me. We have debated the question three or four hours together; but though, in the Pope's name, I have endeavoured to bring over the mind of His Majesty, and reconcile him to the Queen, I have had no more success in persuading the Cardinal than if I had spoken to a rock. His objections are founded on the invalidity of the marriage, the instability of the realm and the succession; and they are so wedded to this opinion that they not only solicit my compliance with them but the expedition of this business with all possible haste."[1]

Convinced that he could do nothing with Wolsey, but determined to attempt to persuade Henry to yield to the Pope's entreaties and resolved to do his duty by attempting to reconcile the King and Queen, Campeggio, though "he could neither ride nor walk and could not sit without discomfort,"[2] was received in audience by Henry on October 22nd, 1528.

Great solemnity attended this reception. We shall not attempt to describe its pageantry, but shall confine our attention to what took place when the King drew the two Legates, Campeggio and Wolsey, into another chamber. It was there, and again the next day, that the Italian Cardinal exhorted Henry against proceeding with the case. To avoid scandal and satisfy the royal conscience it was suggested that a new Dispensation be obtained.

Henry listened patiently but retorted that the

---

[1] Brewer, *op. cit.*, Vol. II, p. 297.
[2] *Ibid.*, p. 298.

marriage was, as he put it, *contra jus divinum* and that no Dispensation could make it valid. He impressed on Campeggio that he had carefully studied the matter, and that, although he insisted that he wanted nothing more than a declaration whether the union was valid or not, " if an angel descended from heaven he would not be able to convince his Majesty " that Catherine was his lawful wife.[1]

Confronted by Wolsey, with whom he had no more success than if he had been addressing a rock, and convinced that Henry was so enamoured of his own theological acumen that an angel from heaven could not persuade him that his marriage was dispensable, Campeggio sought the line of least resistance. The three men, the King and the two Cardinals, discussed a proposal for persuading the Queen to enter some religious house. Before the attempt was made to carry out this frontal attack, the Italian, foreseeing that it might fail, apprised Wolsey that according to the Pope's instructions he was bound to acquaint the Holy See with what was transpiring and await further instructions before proceeding any further.[2]

[1] Brewer, *op. cit.*, Vol. II, p. 299.
[2] *Ibid.*, p. 299.

CHAPTER XI

CATHERINE'S " OBSTINACY "

THE Queen understood the significance of
Campeggio's mission. It told her that if the
sweating sickness had temporarily cooled the ardour
of the King's passion and momentarily cast a damper
upon his " pernicious and inordinate carnal love "[1]
the flame within him had flared up as soon as the
temperature of those surrounding him had again
become normal. When, during the epidemic, she
had seen him, making thirty-nine wills, confessing
his sins every day and sharing in her devout
exercises,[2] she had cherished the illusion that his
" carnal desire and voluptuous affection of foolish
love "[3] had run its course. Campeggio's presence
in England told her, however, that when ambitious
politicians have made up their minds to capitalize
the concupiscence of a lustful man and of an
appetizing damsel, nothing but the fear of imminent
death can arrest the lustful longings aroused,
nurtured and manœuvred by such designing men.

Catherine did not permit her outraged sense of
self-respect to shake her equanimity. The daughter

[1] Cavendish, *op. cit.*, p. 211.
[2] Strickland, Vol. II, p. 539.
[3] Cavendish, *op. cit.*, p. 210.

of Isabella the Catholic, she proved herself worthy of her mother by confronting her Calvary with unruffled serenity of soul. Herbert, who refused to read the records which he consulted except through Henry's lenses,[1] seems to blame her because she refrained from losing her self-composure. He remarks that

" her countenance not only in Court, but to the people was more cheerfull than ordinary ; whereas (it was alleaged) she might be more sad and pensive, considering the King's Conscience was unsatisfied, and that he had refrained her bed, and was not willing the Lady Princess, her Daughter, should come in her Company."[2]

It was in this spirit of placid self-control that the Queen awaited the visit of the two Cardinals. She knew that it could not be long delayed. We suspect that she had an inkling of the nature of the pressure that would be brought to bear upon her. At all events, when Campeggio and Wolsey were received in audience by her she said to them :

" Is it now a question whether I be the King's lawful wife or not, when I have been married to him almost twenty years and no objection made before ? Divers prelates and lords, privy councillors of the King, are yet alive, who then adjudged our marriage good and lawful, and now to say it is detestable is a great marvel to me, especially when I consider what a wise prince the King's father was, and also the

---

[1] *Encyclopædia Britannica, XIII Edition,* verbo Herbert, XII vol., p. 341.
[2] Herbert, *op. cit.,* p. 225.

natural affection my father, King Ferdinand, bare upon me. I think that neither of our fathers were so unwise and weak in judgment but they foresaw what would follow our marriage."[1]

There is an objectivity in this manner of discussing her own case, which shows that Catherine's nerves must have been made of steel and that her self-restraint was perfect. She was then in her forty-fifth year. Spanish women at that age are apt to be highly strung and neurotic, but no English woman could possibly have shown greater poise under trying conditions than did Catherine on that October day of 1528, when she was submitted to this gruelling ordeal.

Calmly and dispassionately the Queen continued in this strain :

" The King, my father, sent to the Court of Rome, and there obtained a Dispensation that I, being the one brother's wife, might without scruple of conscience marry the other brother lawfully, which license, under lead, I have yet to show, which makes me say and surely believe, as my first marriage was not completed, that my second is good and lawful."

But if Catherine thus held her ground and made it perfectly clear that she had her nerves under absolute control, she did not cease to be a woman. She turned to Wolsey and with impeccable courtesy and a slowness of diction that lent emphasis to every word that fell from her lips, said :—

" Of this trouble I may only thank you, my lord

[1] Strickland, *op. cit.*, Vol. II, p. 541.

of York, because I ever wondered at your pride and vain glory, and abhorred your voluptuous life, and little cared for your presumption and tyranny ; therefore of malice have you kindled this fire, especially for the great grudge you bear to my nephew, the Emperor, whom you hate worser than a scorpion, because he would not gratify your ambition by making you Pope by force."

With the Queen in this frame of mind it was useless to seek to reason with her. Campeggio did not attempt to do so. Cardinals are invariably students of human nature. They know when silence is golden. The audience to which we have just referred took place on October 24th, 1528. He returned to the charge three days later and submitted to Rome a report of what then transpired, in which he said that he did not despair of success in persuading Catherine to enter some religious order,[1] or, to quote Froude, " to enter ' lax religion,' to take vows of chastity which, at her age and under her conditions of health, would be a mere form."[2]

It would appear from the staunch Protestant historian to whom we have just referred, that the Queen would perhaps have complied with this suggestion " had the King's plea been confined, as at first, to the political exigencies of the succession. But," he continues, " the open and premature choice of the lady who was to take her place was an indignity not to be borne. She had the pride of her

[1] Brewer, op. cit., Vol. II, p. 302,
[2] Froude, op. cit., p. 77.

race. Her obstinacy was a match for her husband's. She was shaken for a moment by the impassioned entreaties of Campeggio, and she did not at once absolutely refuse. The Legate postponed the opening of his Court. He referred to Rome for further instructions."[1]

We are inclined to believe that both Campeggio and Froude misunderstood Catherine's attitude. Of course, we may be mistaken but our opinion is that they mistook her caution for hesitancy, her self-control for wavering. We say this because she concluded the first conference by saying that she was a lone woman and a stranger without a friend or an adviser, that she intended to ask that counsel be assigned to her and that she would, at a later date, grant the Cardinals another audience.[2] She felt, in a word, that she was defenceless and that her interests required that she refrain from committing herself in any way. But she intimated that when she had been fully apprised of the nature of her rights, she would not hesitate to take whatever stand she considered proper.

It would appear that John Fisher, Bishop of Rochester, whom the Catholic Church canonized in 1935, was placed in charge of her case. Our theory is that he told her that she could not be forced to enter " lax religion " and that when she thus felt secure of her ground she spoke out without hesitation.

The best of fighting blood coursed through her

---

[1] Froude, *op. cit.*, p. 78.
[2] Brewer, *op. cit.*, Vol. II, p. 302.

arteries. It told her to accept the gage of battle.
She was adamant. Wolsey aroused her ire by
holding, in the teeth of her assurance to the contrary,
that Arthur had had carnal knowledge of her. She
affirmed, on her conscience, that from her marriage
on November 14th, 1501, until his death on April
2nd, 1502, her first husband had not slept in the
same bed with her more than seven nights. She,
nevertheless, insisted—and here we quote the Italian
of Campeggio's report to the Papacy—that " *che da
lui è resto intacta et incorrupta come vene dal ventro di
sua madre.*"[1]

We shall not stop to consider the interrogation
marks which this statement may suggest. All that
we shall say is that an anonymous writer who, as
far as we know, is not a Catholic, asserts that
" Campeggio could not disbelieve her, and the
judgment of history, differing somewhat in the
estimate of evidence from the judgment of law,
must, we think, accept her word."[2] What interests
our narrative, at its present stage, is that Catherine,
having made the assertion which we have quoted
and knowing that Wolsey questioned it, would not
have been the daughter of Ferdinand and Isabella
if she had not planted her two feet firmly upon the
ground and refused to budge an inch.

One outstanding consideration arose from
Campeggio's audience with the Queen which had
nothing to do with the intimate details we have just

[1] Brewer, *op. cit.*, Vol. II, p. 303.
[2] *Quarterly Review* for January, 1877, *op. cit.*, p. 37.

mentioned. She had challenged Wolsey's impartiality in a manner which, translated into legal phraseology, means that she insisted upon his recusation.

The various authors, whose works are strewn round us as we write, appear to have taken it for granted that Clement and Campeggio were merely fighting for time and were afraid to do their duty. They see in the fact that the Italian Cardinal, in reporting to Rome the substance of his conversations with the Queen, had asked for further instructions, proof that he was a coward who sought for an escape from the discharge of a disagreeable task. We look at the matter from a different angle. We feel that he would have been false to the spirit of his mandate had he failed to apprise the Pope that Catherine, who was entitled to be judged by an impartial bench, had not only challenged Wolsey but had accused him of being the prime cause of her woes.

Before our point of view be brushed aside it may be well to recall :—

(1) That Wolsey had been apprised, when Campeggio was in Paris on his way to London, that the latter had said that he would not proceed to sentence until he had received a new and express Commission from Rome [1] and

(2) That when Campeggio was first received in audience by Henry he had stated that he was bound to submit a preliminary report to the Pope

[1] Brewer, *op. cit.*, Vol. II, p. 292.

and await further instructions before proceeding to judgment.[1]

Our footnotes show that we base these two statements upon source material placed at our disposal through Brewer's painstaking and scholarly researches. We, nevertheless, read in the selfsame work that :

" This dilatoriness and apparent want of resolution on the part of his colleague was by no means agreeable to Wolsey. Campeggio seemed far more bent on knitting together again the disrupted tie by which the King was still held than in proceeding with the divorce. He was ignorant of the fact that Campeggio's instructions extended no further."[2]

Brewer has asserted in absolute good faith that Wolsey " was ignorant of the fact that Campeggio's instructions extended no further " than to a mandate to seek to reconcile Henry and Catherine. He is equally sincere when he expresses surprise that the Italian Cardinal seemed to be " far more bent on knitting together again the disrupted tie . . . than in proceeding with the divorce." And the other authors whose works are now staring us in the face are equally honest when they disseminate the same inaccurate information.

Wolsey has deliberately led these historians into error in getting them to believe that he was ignorant of the nature of Campeggio's instructions. The fact that they looked at the attempts at reconciliation

[1] Brewer, *op. cit.*, Vol. II, p. 299.
[2] *Ibid.*, p. 304.

L

from the standpoint of the common law and did not consider that of the Canon Law—or of modern French Civil Law—accounts for their second mistake.

We have already explained the first phase of Wolsey's deceit in connection with the Commission given the Legatine Court. We have shown that Gardiner, his agent, like Knight and Casali who had first been sent to Rome, had failed in his mission and had not succeeded in inducing the Pope to give a blank power of attorney to the English Episcopacy to ride rough shod over Catherine. We have stressed the fact that Wolsey sought to hide his failure and to hold on to power by falling back upon the expedient of a " Decretal Bull." We have laboured the point that he saw that neither the Commission nor the " Decretal Bull " made him the master of the situation. And we have added that he dared not tell the truth to Henry and that the Canonists, who as a class belonged to his party, were afraid to speak out and let it be known that their chief was skating on thin ice.

When Wolsey was advised from Paris that Campeggio had there stated that he would not proceed to sentence until he had received another and express Commission from Rome, no new information was conveyed to him He was a Canonist and thoroughly understood the situation. But he was too prudent a man to attempt to do anything. He knew that his hands were tied.

When Campeggio made the selfsame statement, in Wolsey's presence, at his first audience with

Henry, nothing was left for the embarrassed Minister to do but to bide his time and keep quiet lest a discussion enable the King to learn that he was living in a fool's paradise. Wolsey, however, built a fire under Campeggio and sought to compel his colleague to expedite matters as much as possible.

It is because it is a matter of record that the Archbishop of York was importunate in urging Campeggio to proceed that the inference has been drawn which we consider erroneous. We know from Brewer that during a part of the time when this pressure was the greatest the Italian Legate suffered from " an acute attack of gout in the knee and was unable to use it without great agony."[1] We are, nevertheless, told by Burnet that " he led at this time a very dissolute life in England, hunting and gaming all the day long and following whores all the night."[2]

We shall not stop to inquire when Italians, advanced in years, first became addicted to " hunting and gaming all the day long." We shall not ask how any man of any nationality, even in the prime of youth and with no gout to restrain his movements, could ride behind the hounds " all the day long " and run after doves " all the night." We merely refer to the matter to show that somebody—perhaps Wolsey—was so interested in besmirching Campeggio that his gout was temporarily overlooked and he was attributed powers of physical resistance

[1] Brewer, *op. cit.*, Vol. II, p. 302.
[2] Burnet, *op. cit.*, Vol. I, p. 108.

which no Hercules, at the height of his vigour, could have equalled.

There was another aspect of the matter, elicited in the Cardinal's first audience with the Queen, of which Wolsey took due note. It will be recalled that she had said :

" The King, my father, sent to the Court of Rome and there obtained a Dispensation . . . which I have yet to show, which makes me say and surely believe, as my first marriage was not completed, that my second is good and lawful."

This statement bothered Wolsey because it referred to a Dispensation which the Queen had " yet to show." It is true that she added that it " makes me say and surely believe, as my first marriage was not completed, that my second is good and lawful." He feared, nevertheless, that its terms might be broader than those of the Dispensation he had seen. He was worried and desired to get possession of this unseen document. He feared that it might validate the marriage between Henry and Catherine even in the event that Arthur had had carnal knowledge of his wife.

The driving power of Wolsey's case was based on his assumption that he could convince the Legatine Court, that is to say Campeggio and himself, that Arthur and Catherine had consummated their marriage. We have already seen that he had affidavits, or some such proof, that the dowager Duchess of Norfolk and other distinguished partisans of the Norfolk-Suffolk faction would swear that they had seen " Prince Arthur and the Lady Catherine, alone in bed together, the next day after their Marriage."[1] He had heard the Queen herself declare that she and Arthur had slept in the same bed at least seven nights. He argued, with these facts before him, somewhat along these lines :

" Ferdinand of Aragon was a politician and so enamoured of his conceit that he was capable of over-reaching himself. But Isabella of Castille was a woman of unflinching common sense. She may have known from her daughter that Arthur had been too young for marriage and that Catherine had been a wife in name only but she may well have said that the Dispensation which Ferdinand had accepted may some day give rise to a question of fact which should be ruled out before it can be raised. Should political reasons ever dictate an attack upon the union of Henry and Catherine, this question of fact would obviously come to the fore. The innocent wife must be protected against any and all such contingencies by a second Dispensation."

Wolsey's keen mind saw the possibilities which we have compressed into the reasoning thus attributed to Queen Isabella. He determined to find out in Rome whether any such second Dispensation existed, and, if it did, to suppress it by fair means or foul.

Wolsey's campaign to get rid of Catherine had been based upon his interpretation of the Dispensation submitted to him by Henry. He had construed its

---

[1] Herbert, *op. cit.*, p. 242.

text as implying that the Pope took it for granted that Arthur had not had carnal knowledge of Catherine. The existence of a second Dispensation, of which the Cardinal had not been apprised, played havoc with his plans. He feared that it might have given Henry permission to marry Catherine even if Arthur and she had consummated their union. This was why he was in such mortal dread of the production of this new exhibit.

We thus read in Burnet that " in the beginning of December (1528) Sir Francis Brian and Peter Vannes, the King's Secretary for the Latin tongue, were sent to Rome. They had it in the commission to search all the records there for the Breve (the second Dispensation) now so much talked of in Spain."[1] These Ambassadors had other instructions which the same author thus summarizes :

" They were to propose several overtures : whether if the Queen vowed religion, the Pope would not dispense with the King's second marriage ? Or, if the Queen would not vow religion unless the King also did it, whether in that case would the Pope dispense with his vow ? Or whether, if the Queen would hear of no such proposition, would not the Pope dispense with the King's having two wives, for which there were divers precedents vouched from the Old Testament."[2]

True to the practice, which we have noted in the past, these demands were backed up by threats.

---

[1] Burnet, *op. cit.*, Vol. I, p. 94.
[2] *Ibid.*, p. 94.

Brian and Vannes were instructed to represent to the Pope that " the King had laid out much of his best treasure in the Papal service and that he expected the highest favours out of the deepest treasures of the Church." Such language savoured more of a hint than of a menace. But Vannes was " also commanded to tell the Pope, as of himself, that if for partial respects and fears the King's desires were refused, he perceived it would not only alienate the King but that many other princes, his confederates, with their realms, would withdraw their devotion and obedience from the Apostolic See."[1]

When it was seen that Brian and Vannes could not get what they desired, three other delegates Knight, Bennet and Taylor, were dispatched to Rome with orders to let it be known that the King would be sorry if it were not shown that the second Bull of Dispensation was a forgery.[2] Henry had, in the meantime, prevailed upon Catherine to have a copy of this document brought to England from Spain. In doing so he resorted to practices which Brewer characterizes as infamous, adding that if Henry " himself was not the author of the deceit he became the willing witness in deceiving his consort."[3]

We may be mistaken, but we place the primary blame upon Wolsey, not upon the King. Henry's passions were aroused and, for " pernicious and inordinate carnal love," men often subordinate

---

[1] Burnet, *op. cit.*, Vol. I, p. 95.
[2] Brewer, *op. cit.*, Vol. II, p. 313.
[3] *Ibid.*, p. 308.

their better instincts to their lust. As throughout
the matter he was the dupe of the Cardinal and of
the Norfolks, who used him for their unavowable
ends, there is no reason to believe that in this
particular instance he acted upon his own initiative
The production of that second Dispensation before
the trial, so that Wolsey could prepare to attempt to
tear it to pieces, was essential to the success of the
cause which he was directing as Henry's chief
counsel and which he desired to judge as the Pope's
representative.

CHAPTER XII

THE SECOND DISPENSATION

HENRY and Wolsey would not have gone to such lengths in their endeavours to do away with this second Dispensation if they had not felt that its admission in evidence would have been fatal to their cause. They admitted the power of the Pope to grant a Dispensation provided it did not interfere with what they considered the divine inhibition decreed by Holy Writ. They tacitly conceded that a marriage, according to Canon Law, is not really a marriage until it is consummated. They based their entire case on their ability to prove that Arthur had had carnal knowledge of Catherine.

This second Breve, which it was claimed that Isabella of Castille had obtained from the Pope in amplification of the first one, was said to differ from the original document in two essential particulars. Faithful to our policy of making but few statements of fact ourselves and of having the Pope's point of view set forth, as far as possible, by well-known Protestant authorities, we shall let the author of the *History of the Reformation* tell us of these distinctions. He writes :

" For whereas in the Bull (the first one) the

preamble bore, that the King and Queen had desired the Pope's Dispensation to marry, that the peace might continue between the two crowns, without any other cause being given ; in the preamble of this Breve (the second one) mention is made of their desire to marry because otherwise it was not likely that the peace would be continued between the two crowns : and for that, and divers other reasons they asked the Dispensation."[1]

The second major difference is thus set forth by Burnet :

" In the Bull (the first one) it is only said, that the Queen's petition bore : ' That *perhaps* she had consummated her marriage with Prince Arthur by the *carnalis copula.*' But in this (the second Bull) *perhaps* is left out, and it is plainly said, that they had consummated their marriage."

The text of the first draft had been due to the fact that Ferdinand of Aragon had assured Julius II that Prince Arthur was too young for marriage and that Catherine, during her short union with a failing invalid, had not contracted the supposed affinity. The Dispensation had been granted by the Pope with these representations acting as a major consideration.[2] Isabella of Castille had subsequently insisted on a second Dispensation being issued. She did so for reasons which we have already explained and which amply demonstrate her clearness of vision and her almost uncanny common sense.

---

[1] Burnet, *op. cit.*, Vol. I, p. 89.
[2] *Quarterly Review*, January, 1877, p. 27.

As we write these lines we can recall no Common Law term that describes the procedure resorted to by Henry to keep this second Dispensation out of the record. A modern French civilian would illustrate what took place by saying that "*Il s'est inscrit en faux contre la pièce*." This means that he opposed the admissibility of this Bull in evidence on the ground that it was a forgery and that he asked that the usual procedure incident to an *inscription en faux* should be followed. The upshot of this was that an inquiry was ordered, or at all events carried on, to ascertain whether this exhibit was genuine or not.

While this ancillary investigation was going on Wolsey suddenly found himself in a most awkward position. Word reached him that Clement VII was dying. This news fanned his ever-present ambition to discard his red hat for the Papal tiara. He had striven to do so when Leo X passed away in 1521. He was ready, as he then declared, to pay 100,000 ducats in order to reach this goal. Henry besieged Charles V with formal entreaties to intervene in his behalf.[1] When Adrian VI died in 1523, he was again a candidate. Henry and he once more actively canvassed for his election.[2] The Emperor probably laughed at their importunities and said to himself " these men must have nerves of brass to ask my aid when they are engaged in a conspiracy to humiliate my aunt."

[1] Pastor, *op. cit.*, Vol. IX., p. 7.
[2] *Ibid.*, p. 231.

Let us pause for a moment, even at the risk of breaking the continuity of our thoughts, to contemplate the part that this refusal by Charles to favour the realization of Wolsey's ambition may have played in engendering Henry's " scrupulosity of conscience." We learnt, as late as the death of Leo XIII in 1903, that the veto of the Austrian Emperor, expressed through the Cardinal of Cracow, played havoc with Rampolla's ambitions. Wolsey read the handwriting on the wall when he scrutinized the votes cast in 1523. He saw that the Emperor was unalterably opposed to him and that that meant that he was faced by an almost insurmountable difficulty.

If we compare our dates and recall that Clement was elected Pope in 1523 and that Henry's retreat from Catherine's bed took place in 1524, are we not justified in asking ourselves whether this awakening of the King's conscience at so late an hour was not a sequel to Wolsey's hatred of the Emperor and part of his plan of encircling Spain and of working towards an Anglo-French alliance cemented by family ties and made possible by jettisoning Catherine and replacing her by a French princess ?

Of course, this is mere conjecture. We are impressed, however, by the circumstance that Wolsey's mind was centred upon the Papacy at the very time when this *procédure d'inscription en faux* should have been under headway. We therefore have no difficulty in agreeing with Brewer that "in this state of things to obtain from the Pope any decision on the forgery of the Brief . . . was out of the question. The attention of all men was exclusively turned in one direction—the immediate death of the Pope and the nomination of his successor."[1]

Clement refused to gratify Wolsey or anybody else by dying. He lived on, and remained true to his principles.[2] So adamant was he that Vannes wrote to the King that nothing could be accomplished " for, if the Queen entered religion, the Pope, according to the learned at Rome, could not grant a Dispensation to the King to marry again."[3]

This intransigent attitude of the Holy See had as its logical consequence the necessity of going on with the trial before a Court dominated not by Wolsey but by Campeggio, and acting under a Commission which Wolsey knew full well did not tie the Pope's hands or in any way prevent the " revocation " of the case. And this alternative of dropping the matter or accepting to plead before a bench which was personified by its presiding officer, carried with it the corollary of forcing Anne to abandon the luxurious apartment that she occupied at Greenwich. Wolsey deemed it impolitic that she and Henry should offend public decency when the judges were about to convene to hear the King's case.

It appears that the time had now passed when

---

[1] Brewer, *op. cit.*, Vol. II, p. 328.
[2] *Ibid.*, p. 331.
[3] *Ibid.*, p. 332.

Anne's " constant virginity " was the stock-in-trade of the Norfolk faction.   The poet asks :

> " What can ennoble sots or slaves or cowards ?
>   Alas. Not all the blood of all the Howards."

In this particular instance the Howard strain—Anne Boleyn's mother was a Howard—appears to have broken under the stress of attempting to play indefinitely the impossible part of an immaculate Delilah to a red-bearded and persistent Samson. At all events, Brewer records that when the date of the trial drew near, the nature of the relations between her and the King could scarcely be doubted. Henry's " unrestrained access to her apartment *sine arbitris*," is the way he brings out this fact, " more than once hinted at in his letters, leads to but one conclusion."[1]

The Catholic Church teaches her children that they must avoid not only evil but the appearance of evil.   It may be that the Norfolks—the Howards—were so astute in maintaining unimpaired their hold upon Henry that they did not permit him to possess Anne even when he and she were *sine arbitris*.   The politicians may have used this freedom of access as a decoy and have protected their quarry by an unexpected interruption at the psychological moment.   They and she may have had a preconcerted system of signals of which Henry was kept in blissful ignorance.   When political schemers and an ambitious woman see eye to eye all things are possible.

[1] Brewer, *op. cit.*, Vol. II, p. 316.

Whatever may or not have taken place when the curtains of that apartment at Greenwich were drawn, the appearance of evil was not avoided. The fears of the retainers of the Norfolk faction were aroused. They were afraid of public opinion. They dreaded that something might happen which would outrage public decency. Their thoughts were centred upon Anne's waistline. Here is an extract from a letter, written in sixteenth-century French by a man who listened and who kept his eyes open :

"*Je ne doubte fort que depuis quelque ce Roy ait approché bien pres de Mademoiselle Anne : car si le ventre croist, tout sera gasté.*"[1]

When all the delays born (a) of Wolsey's sending Ambassador after Ambassador to Rome to have the Commission of the Legatine Court modified, (b) of what we shall call his "*inscription en faux contre* the Second Dispensation" and (c) of his desire to enlist the Emperor's support to make him Pope, had held up Campeggio in England for eight and a half months—from October 1st, 1528, to June 18th, 1529—it became obvious that the trial could no longer be postponed. Anne's relations with Henry had manifestly reached a point which made any further delay dangerous to the King's cause. Wolsey could procrastinate no longer. He had to let matters take their course and risk everything in the hope of gaining everything.

---

[1] Brewer, *op. cit.*, Vol. II, p. 316 (note).

Catherine had not been treated fairly during the months when Wolsey would willingly have sacrificed Henry if Charles had assured him of the Papacy. His inordinate ambition knew no bounds and we fear that even loyalty would not have restrained him if the tiara had been the price of his fidelity. It should not be forgotten that his code of ethics was what Alexander Pope had in view when he asked :

" What can ennoble sots or slaves or cowards ? "

Henry, however, was a Tudor and his allies in this fight against a Spanish woman had " all the blood of all the Howards."   It is thus with surprise that we learn that Catherine was not allowed to choose counsel to defend her rights.   She protested to Campeggio against this manifest injustice telling him that she was left without advisers, and that though certain Englishmen had been appointed her counsellors by the King, it was easy to believe, she said, that they would rather consult their royal master's pleasure " than regard what was most conducive to her interests."[1]

Whatever may have been the reasons which caused Henry and the nobles to whom Catherine's very name had become anathema, to forget that fundamental rule of English fair play to which we have just referred, the King on May 31st, 1529, " by a warrant under the great seal gave the Legates (Campeggio and Wolsey) leave to execute their Commission, upon which they sate that same day."[2]

---

[1] Brewer, *op. cit.*, Vol. II, p. 339.
[2] Burnet, *op. cit.*, Vol. I, p. 112.

The Commission was presented by Longland, Bishop of Lincoln. It was given to the Protonotary of the Court and he read it publicly. The Legates took it in their hands and declared that they were resolved to execute it. The clerks of the Court were then sworn in and peremptory citations were addressed to the King and Queen ordering them to appear at Blackfriars on June 18th, 1529, between nine and ten o'clock. Adjournment followed.[1]

The terms of this citation caused George Cavendish, Wolsey's " Gentleman Usher," to describe them as :

" the strangest and newest sight and device that ever was read or heard in any history or chronicle in any region : that a King and a Queen should be convented and constrained by proces compellatory to appear in any Court as common persons, within their own realm or dominion, to abide the judgment and decrees of their own subjects, having the royal diadem and prerogative thereof."[2]

And growing introspective in his language Cavendish added :

" Is it not a world to consider the desire of wilful princes, when they fully be bent and inclined to fulfil their voluptuous appetites, against the which no reasonable persuasions will suffice ; little or nothing weighing or regarding the dangerous sequel that doth ensue to themselves as to their realm and subjects. And above all things, there is no one

---

[1] Burnet, *op. cit.*, Vol. I, p. 112.
[2] Cavendish, *op. cit.*, p. 210.

M

thing that causeth them to be more wilful than carnal desire and voluptuous affection of foolish love."

A solemn Court was prepared in the great hall of the palace at Blackfriars. Campeggio and Wolsey had each a chair of cloth of gold placed before a table covered with rich tapestry. There was also " a cloth of estate under which sat the King ; and the Queen sat some distance beneath the King ; under the judges feet sat the officers of the Court. The Chief Scribe there was Dr. Stephens[1] (who was after Bishop of Winchester) ; the apparitor was one Cooke, most commonly called Cooke of Winchester. Then sat there, within the said Court, directly before the King and the judges, the Archbishop of Canterbury, Doctor Warham, and all the other Bishops. Then at both the ends, with a bar made for them, the counsellors on both sides."[2]

The Canonists who appeared for the King were Doctor Sampson, who subsequently became Bishop of Chichester, and Doctor Bell, who, at a later date, was Bishop of Worcester. They had an array of assistants. The King's proctors were Doctor Peter, who afterwards was the King's chief secretary, Doctor Tregonell and a corps of aides.

On the other side of the bar stood Doctor Fisher, Bishop of Rochester whom Cavendish calls " a very godly man and a devout person, who after suffered death at Tower Hill ; the which was greatly lamented

---

[1] Dr. Stephen Gardiner. It will be recalled that he was sent to Orvieto by the King and Wolsey.
[2] Cavendish, *op. cit.*, p. 212.

through all the foreign universities of Christendom."[1]
His associates were Doctor Standish, some time a
Grey Friar, and then Bishop of St. Asaph in Wales,
and Doctor Ridley, " a very small person in stature,
but surely a great and an excellent clerk in divinity."

When we turn to Froude we learn that as soon as
the Court was called to order one of Henry's
proctors said that the King had scruples about the
validity of his marriage which he required to be
resolved.   Catherine attended in person.   She
delivered a brief protest against the place of trial
and the partiality of the judges, stressing the point
that Campeggio held an English Bishopric and that
Wolsey was the King's subject.

Reply was made that Henry could not plead in a
city where the Emperor was master.   This objection
was based upon the fact that the Imperial troops
then dominated the Papal States.   The Court
adjourned for three days in order to consider these
points.[2]

When proceedings were resumed on June 21st,
1529, the scene became more solemn and imposing.
Henry came in person and took his place under a
canopy at the right of the Legates.   Catherine again
appeared and sat in equal state on their left.   When
the judges had commanded the crier to proclaim
silence, the summons : " King Henry of England,
come into Court," rang through the hall.   " Here,
my Lords," was the answer.

[1] Cavendish, *op. cit.*, p. 213.
[2] Froude, *op. cit.*, p. 101.

When the bailiff cried, " Catherine, Queen of England, come into Court," she who was thus summoned made no answer. On the contrary, she " rose up incontintent out of her chair, where as she sat, and because she could not come directly to the King for the distance which severed them, she took pain to go about unto the King, kneeling down at his feet in the sight of all the Court and assembly, to whom she said, in effect, in broken English, as followeth :

" ' Sir,' quoth she, ' I beseech you for all the love that hath been between us, let me have justice and right, take of me some pity and compassion for I am a poor woman and a stranger born out of your dominion.   I have here no assured friend, and much less indifferent counsel.   I flee to you as to the head of justice within this realm.' "[1]

Catherine had heard that at a recent meeting of the King's Council a note had been drafted in Wolsey's hand which read : " The substance of it is that they were informed some designed to kill the King or the Cardinal . . . and she had not shewed much love to the King, neither in bed nor out of bed as she ought.   And now that the King was very pensive, and in much grief, she shewed great signs of joy, setting on all people to dancings and other diversions."[2]

The Queen paid no attention to the first and third of these charges.   She spoke in this strain to the

[1] Cavendish, *op. cit.*, p. 213.
[2] Burnet, *op. cit.*, Vol. I, p. 113.

second, in which she was accused of lacking in affection :

" I take God and all the world to witness, that I have been to you a true, humble and obedient wife, ever conforming to your will and pleasure, that never said or did anything to the contrary thereof, being always well pleased and contented with all things wherein you had delight or dalliance, whether it were in little or much. . . . This twenty years, I have been your true wife or more, and by me ye have had divers children, although it hath pleased God to call them out of this world which hath been no default in me."[1]

And then going straight to the subject that rankled in her soul, taking up the gage of battle by which Wolsey, the son of a butcher, sought to give the lie to her, she, the daughter of a race of Kings and Queens, always addressing not the Court but Henry, added :

" And when ye had me at the first, I take God to be my judge, I was a true maid without touch of man ; and whether it be true or no, I put it to your conscience. If there be any just cause by the law that ye can allege against me, either of dishonesty or any other impediment to banish and put me from you, I am well content to depart to my shame and dishonour ; and if there be none, then here I most lowly beseech you let me remain in my former estate, and receive justice at your hands. . . . Therefore I most humbly require you, in the way of charity, and for the love of God, who is

[1] Cavendish, *op. cit.*, p. 215.

the just judge, to spare me the extremity of this new Court, until I may be advertised what way and order my friends in Spain will advise me to take. And if ye will not extend to me so much indifferent favour, your pleasure then be fulfilled, and to God I commit my cause."[1]

The Queen meant exactly what she had said. She was prepared to kneel before her husband and to entreat him to let her have " right and justice " and take of her " some pity and compassion," but she was determined not to stand in justice before a bench on which sat a plebeian who had sought to browbeat her and who doubted her plighted word. When she had finished her plea to Henry she arose and making a low curtsy to him, but ignoring the existence of the Court, departed " from thence."[2] She took her way straight out of the palace of Blackfriars.

Crowds of women, gathered around the entrance gates, had cheered her as she had entered and had bade her care for nothing. If women had to decide the case, said the French Ambassador, the Queen would win. " Their voices availed nothing," retorts Froude.[3] She did not place her trust in them. She put it in a still higher power. But she accepted their applause with quiet dignity when it again greeted her on her departure. She knew that if men were about to do her wrong, her own sex was true to her.

When Henry perceived that Catherine had left the Court room, forgetting that he was but an

---

[1] Cavendish, *op. cit.*, p. 215.
[2] *Ibid.*, p. 217.
[3] Froude, *op. cit.*, p. 102.

ordinary party to an action at law, he commanded
the crier to call her. The summons " Catherine,
Queen of England, come into Court," again
resounded through the hall. Master Griffith who
heard this order said : " Madam, ye be called
again." " Go on," quoth she, " it maketh no matter,
for it is no indifferent Court for me ; therefore,
I will not tarry. Go on your ways." [1]

When Henry was convinced that Catherine had
no intention of returning he arose and said :

" For as much as the Queen is gone, I will, in her
absence, declare unto you all my Lords here presently
assembled, she hath been to me as true, as obedient
and as conformable a wife as I could in my fantasy
wish or desire. She hath all the virtuous qualities
that ought to be in a woman of her dignity, or in
any other of baser estate. Surely she is also a noble
woman born, if nothing were in her, but only her
conditions will well declare the same."[2]

These remarks frightened Wolsey. He thought
that Henry had been won over by Catherine's plea
or that something had gone wrong. He hastened
to ask the King whether he had been the inventor
or mover of this suit. This inquiry accomplished
the result the Cardinal had in view. It revived
Henry's fighting blood. It met with the reply that
Wolsey had been against the proposal and that it
was the King's " scrupulosity of conscience " and
nothing else that had started the entire matter.

[1] Cavendish, *op. cit.*, p. 218.
[2] *Ibid.*, p. 218.

CHAPTER XIII

THE TRIAL

LET us see just what Henry himself has to say about his "scrupulosity of conscience." Cavendish claims to have been present at the trial. His recital of what took place may not be a verbatim report of what occurred. It is, nevertheless, a contemporary report of the proceedings. The King began in this vein :

" And to put you all out of doubt, I will declare unto you the special cause that moved me hereunto ; it was a certain scrupulosity that pricked my conscience upon divers words that were spoken at a certain time by the Bishop of Bayonne, the French King's Ambassador, who had been here long upon the debating for the conclusion of a marriage to be concluded between the Princess our daughter Mary and the Duke of Orleans, the French King's second son."[1]

Legrand, in his *Histoire du Divorce de Henri VIII*, denies that any such statement was ever made by the French Ambassador, who, it may be remarked parenthetically, was not Bishop of Bayonne but of Tarbes. Both places are in that part of France now known as *les Basses Pyrénées*. Wolsey's secretary was a little out in his geography.

[1] Cavendish, *op. cit.*, p. 219.

168

Even so, we see no reason why he should have invented what he has recorded. His tale rings true. Our opinion is that Legrand bases his affirmation upon the fact that he found no proof, in the official archives consulted by him, that the French Ambassador had used the language upon which Henry placed such stress.

We are inclined to believe that the Bishop of Tarbes purposely refrained from mentioning the matter in his reports to his Foreign Office because it formed part of the unavowable plan that he and the Archbishop of York had evolved to get Henry into their meshes. It is a well-known fact that diplomatic officers sometimes leave no official trace of delicate missions undertaken by them. The Bishop may well have desired to suppress all evidence of his part in this unsavoury matter.

Whether the Bishop of Tarbes made the statement imputed to him by the King is foreign to the issue with which we are concerned.[1] We are dealing with the facts which were submitted to the Legatine Court. We are seeking to understand the Pope's appreciation of them. We are endeavouring to look at Henry's first divorce from Clement's point of view. It is admitted by everybody that whether the French Ambassador's name was used in vain or not, the King made it clear that :

" These words (questioning Mary's legitimacy) were so conceived within my scrupulous conscience,

---

[1] Froude says that " the Bishop of Tarbes was unquestionably the first person to bring the question publicly forward, *op. cit.*, p. 31.

that they bred a doubt within my breast, which doubt pricked, vexed and troubled so my mind, and so disquieted me, that I was in great doubt of God's indignation ; which (as seemed me) appeared right well ; much the rather for that He hath not sent me any issue male ; for all such issue male as I have received of the Queen died incontinent after they were born ; so that I doubt the punishment of God in that behalf."[1]

Having thus described to his judges his state of mind Henry went on to explain why it was that he felt constrained to act. He said :

" Thus being troubled in waves of a scrupulous conscience, and partly in dispair of any issue male by her, it drave me at last to consider the estate of this realm, and the danger it stood in for lack of issue male to succeed me in this imperial dignity. I thought it good, therefore, in relief of the weighty burden of scrupulous conscience, and the quiet estate of this noble realm, to attempt the law therein, and whether I might take another wife in case that my first copulation with this gentlewoman were not lawful ; which I intend not for carnal concupiscence ne for any displeasure or mislike of the Queen's person or age, with whom I could be as well content to continue during my life, if our marriage may stand with God's laws, as with any woman alive ; in which point consisteth all this doubt that we go now about to try by the learned wisdom of you our

[1] Cavendish, *op. cit.*, p. 219.

prelates and pastors of this realm here assembled for that purpose."

As far as we have been able to ascertain, Henry had filed no formal petition setting forth the relief for which he prayed. He had originally been cited, as we have already seen, by the Archbishops of Canterbury and York to appear before them on May 17th, 1527 " to answer for eighteen years' sinful cohabitation with Catherine." Nothing came of that collusive suit.

Two years had passed since then. The present case was, in its final analysis, a replica of the first one, except that it was conducted with greater pomp and solemnity and was carried on contradictorily with Catherine. But we find nothing that tends to show that the King made any statement of the nature of his demands and of the end he envisaged other than what is set forth in the address which we have thought best to reproduce in full.

The conclusion has then been thrust upon us that the Legatine Court was not asked to annul Henry's marriage. It was merely requested to ease Henry's conscience by inquiring into the validity of his union. If we take him at his word, what he desired, as he stood at that bar on June 21st, 1529, was that his judges should relieve the strain upon his soul by giving their approval to the bonds of love that linked him to the mother of his daughter.

We know, however, that while he may have told the Legatine Court that neither " carnal concupiscence " nor " any displeasure or dislike of the

Queen's person or age " had anything to do with his " scrupulosity of conscience," and that while that statement may have been true in regard to the inception of his misgivings, it was a dishonest representation of his state of mind at the time he spoke.

The words which we have just heard Henry pronounce give no indication of the characteristics—aggressive personality, accentuated sexual tendencies, dominant will—which are generally associated with him. On the contrary, they reveal him to us as a dissimulator and as a weakling who, shaken by Catherine's unflinching attitude, had not the backbone to stand up and say what he had intended to say when he entered the Court room.

We have already observed how Wolsey had turned Henry's thoughts from the old alliance with Spain and had made him think of wedding a Tudor to a Valois. We have also taken note of how the designing Norfolks and the willing Anne had sought to circumvent this move by appealing to the King's lust and by abstaining from gratifying it. We now see him forgetting higher politics and what he calls "carnal concupiscence" because he quailed before the Queen's righteous indignation.

A judge must deal with a case as it is defined by the pleadings and as it is established by the evidence. Let us forget about Wolsey, because his conduct in accepting a Commission to pass judgment upon the merits of a controversy in which he had acted as counsel is far too reprehensible to merit consider-

ation. We know that the Papacy had relegated him
to the inferior part of an " assessor " and that
Campeggio eventually took the entire conduct of
the matter into his hands. We, therefore, regard the
Italian Cardinal as the sole embodiment of the
Legatine authority and as incorporating the Papal
jurisdiction. It is for this reason that we have just
spoken of " a judge " and not of " judges " in the
plural.

It was Campeggio's duty to deal with Henry's
demands as defined in the address of which we have
just spoken. It would have been improper for him
to have gone beyond their purview. In endeavouring to make out his case, to prove how anxious he
was to be permitted to return to the Queen's
embraces the King said :

" Wherein after I once perceived my conscience
wounded with the doubtful case herein, I moved
first this matter in confession to you, my Lord of
Lincoln, my ghostly father. And for as much as
then yourself were in some doubt to give me counsel,
moved me to ask farther counsel of all you lords ;
wherein I moved you first my Lord of Canterbury,
axing your license (for as much as you were our
Metropolitan) to put this matter in question ; and
so I did of all you my lords, to the which ye have
all granted by writing under all your seals, the which
I have here to be showed."[1]

We need not stress the importance of this evidence.
It deals with the point at issue. It means that the

---

[1] Cavendish, *op. cit.*, p. 221.

King asserted that all the Bishops of his realm considered that this marriage was invalid. He thought that he was a theologian. He agreed with them but he wished to have their opinion confirmed by a solemn judgment. He feared to live with Catherine without the formal sanction of the Legatine Court.

As soon as this important statement had been made the Archbishop of Canterbury rose and said: " That is truth, if it please your highness. I doubt not but all brethren here present will affirm the same." The unanimity vouched for by the Primate of England met this outburst from the Bishop of Rochester, from him who is now Saint John Fisher. " No, Sir, not I. Ye have not my consent thereto."

We know who it was who used such emphatic language. It was the prelate whom Wolsey had attempted to deceive when he was making the inquiry which grew out of the collusive suit. It was the Churchman whom such a convinced anti-Catholic as Froude describes as " the aged Bishop of Rochester reputed the holiest and wisest of them."[1] It was the theologian who appeared as chief counsel for the Queen.

The King was in absolute good faith when he had said that all his Bishops had given written opinions to the effect that his marriage was invalid. It was for this reason that, instead of being abashed as he had been when Catherine had defied him, he hastened to exclaim : " No ! Look here upon this

[1] Froude, *op. cit.*, p. 34.

is not this your hand and seal ? " showing him at the same time " the instrument with seals."[1]

We shall let Cavendish tell us in his own words what then occurred. His report reads :

" ' No forsooth, Sire,' quoth the Bishop of Rochester, ' it is not my hand nor seal.' To that quoth the King to my Lord of Canterbury, ' Sir, how say ye, is it not his hand and seal ? ' ' Yes, Sir,' quoth my Lord of Canterbury. ' That is not so " quoth the Bishop of Rochester, ' for indeed you were in hand with me to have both my hand and seal, as other of my lords had already done ; but then I said to you, that I would never consent to no such act, for it were much against my conscience ; nor my hand and seal should never be seen at any such instrument, God willing, with much more matter touching the same communication between us.' "[2]

No denial of signature could have been more categorical than that which Fisher threw at Warham. The Primate was staggered, but, as our text puts it, he said : " You say truth ; such words ye said unto me ; but at the last ye were fully persuaded that I should for you subscribe your name, and put to a seal myself, and ye would allow the same."[3]

This retort does not ring true. When the Archbishop of Canterbury admitted that the Bishop of Rochester had spoken the truth and that he had said, at their interview, " my hand and seal should never be seen at any such instrument, with much

[1] Cavendish, *op. cit.*, p. 222.
[2] *Ibid.*, p. 222.
[3] *Ibid.*, p. 222.

more matter touching the same communication between us," it seems highly improbable that so outspoken a man would have agreed to a transparent subterfuge. Cowards fall back upon such expedients. John Fisher was not a coward. He showed that he was not when he replied to his hierarchical superior : " All which words and matters, under your correction my Lord, and supportation of this noble audience, there is no thing more untrue." Henry saw what this language implied. He hastened to exclaim :

" Well, well, it shall make no matter ; we will not stand with you in argument herein, for you are but one man."[1] And with that the Court was adjourned until the next day.

This first hearing throws great light upon the true inwardness of the entire case. It shows how anxious were Wolsey and the ecclesiastical politicians who gravitated in his wake to impress upon Henry that his marriage ran counter to the Levitical prohibition. The Emperor had on two occasions lent his influence to anti-Wolsey candidates in the Papal Conclave. Wolsey knew that he could never become Pope while Charles V remained the dominant factor in Europe. It was only by a close alliance with France that he could hope to realize his ambition. As long as Catherine of Aragon continued to be Queen of England that end could not be accomplished.

It was easy to play upon the superstitions of wha

[1] Cavendish, *op. cit.*, p. 223.

some would call a half-baked theologian. And this was what Henry really was. That was why it was so important to have all these certificates affirming the invalidity of his marriage. They were the arguments, the form of pressure that Wolsey needed in order to break the power of the Emperor and to consolidate an Anglo-French alliance which would curb the influence of Catherine's nephew.

The intriguers then in power knew of the overshadowing influence of the Bishop of Rochester. He was popular, respected and well known. We feel tempted to quote Scott's lines when we speak of him and to say that

> " One blast upon his bugle horn
> Were worth a thousand men."

We mean by this that his seal and signature outweighed all the others put together, and not only in the effect that they would have upon the King but upon public opinion. France was not popular in England during the sixteenth century. Everybody loved the Queen. A Franco-English alliance met with no response from the nation. It was thus imperative that John Fisher's signature and seal should be appended to these statements, so that the King should know where he stood. Had they not been there all the other names would not have carried any weight.

Nobody foresaw that the clumsy forgery which the Bishop of Rochester denounced in open Court would ever be made public. It was taken for

N

granted that the incriminating document would be seen and read by the King and would then be hidden away somewhere or conveniently destroyed. Had Catherine not pricked Henry's "scrupulosity of conscience" he would never have risen that day in Court and have made the assertion which provoked the unwary affirmation of the Archbishop and the unequivocal denunciation of the Bishop who is now a Saint.

The falsification of Fisher's signature and seal had already served its purpose before the spurious document was produced in Court. The forgery had not been uttered to make out a case before a bench of judges but to convince the hesitant, the doubting, the wavering Henry that he could no longer live with Catherine as man and wife. If, when his mind was still in a plastic shape, he had not found the signature and seal of the venerable and beloved Bishop of Rochester appended to one of these statements, he would not have proceeded with the case. He would have asked for an explanation which would have resulted in Fisher being summoned into the royal presence.

We know enough of the Bishop to be certain that he would have defined his position fully, frankly and convincingly. The value of all the other signatures and the weight of all the other seals would not have resisted the driving power of Fisher's personal appeal. And Henry, like all the Tudors, loved popularity. He would not have risked the favour of the public by courting a controversy with the most beloved of English Churchmen. He would have receded from his position, if carnal concupiscence had not then already gained its mastery over him. And we have no proof that it had.

We take it that it is obvious that the crime committed by the Archbishop of Canterbury played a dominant part in winning over the weak Henry. The King's mind, we repeat, was in a fluid state when this forged paper was submitted to him. The mould had been made ; the crucible had been filled but the material in it had not yet hardened. But it had become a solid block when the villainy was denounced. It was then too late for the discovery of the fraud to have any effect because the harm had already been done. The seductions of Anne had by that time been used by another group of politicians to accomplish something which unworthy theologians acting alone might not have been able to bring about.

When the Court convened the next day Catherine did not appear. She had appealed to Henry's honour and challenged the competence of the Tribunal. She refused any further to recognize its existence. The King's legal advisers saw that he had made a mistake in thrusting his personality to the fore. They were men trained in the law. They had no difficulty in perceiving that his statement of his case had not set forth what he really desired. But they knew that his judicial admissions were binding upon them and that nothing that they could say could delete his words from the record.

It does not require a vivid imagination to know

that the King's counsel argued that the marriage was not good from the beginning because of the carnal knowledge which Arthur had had of Catherine. This allegation, upon which they laid great stress, was denied by those who still appeared, we shall not say as representatives of the Queen, who had retired from the case, but as *amici curiæ*. To prove their point Henry's proctor's "alleged many coloured reasons and similitudes of truth."[1]

It was suggested, in the course of the discussion, that counsel were impinging on so delicate a ground and on a subject of so intimate a nature that "no man could know the truth." This remark caused the Bishop of Rochester to exclaim "*Ego nosco veritatem*, I know the truth." The question at once came from the bench : "How know you the truth ?"

We shall let Cavendish pick up the thread of the narrative for us. He thus transcribes what took place, beginning with Fisher's answer :

"'Forsooth, my Lord,' quoth he, '*Ego sum professor veritatis*, I know that God is truth itself, nor He never spake but truth ; who saith, *quos Deus conjunxit, homo non separet*. And foreasmuch as this marriage was made and joined by God to a good intent, I say that I know the truth ; the which cannot be broken or loosen by the power of man upon no feigned occasion." '[2]

It is obvious that the King's representatives could

[1] Cavendish, *op. cit.*, p. 223.
Ibid., p. 224.

not agree to what the Bishop of Rochester had said. Fisher propounded the well-known principle " that what God hath joined together let no man rent asunder." He overlooked the fact that this suit had been brought not as an action envisaging a divorce but to test whether there had ever been a valid marriage, that is to say whether God had ever joined Henry and Catherine in lawful wedlock.

We are not surprised to learn that this ruling came from the Bench :

" So much doth all faithful men know, as well as you. Yet this reason is not sufficient in this case ; for the King's counsel doth allege divers presumptions, to prove the marriage is not good at the beginning, *ergo*, say they it is not joined by God at the beginning and therefore it is not lawful. . . . To say that the matrimony was joined of God, ye must prove it farther than by that text which ye have alleged for your matter for ye must first avoid the presumptions."[1]

This ruling was interpreted as meaning that the Court would admit evidence to prove that Arthur had had carnal knowledge of Catherine, and Doctor Ridley, the " very small person in stature but surely a great and excellent clerk in divinity " to whom we have already referred, at once said : " It is a shame and a great dishonour to this honourable presence, that any such presumptions should be alleged in this open Court, which be to all good and honest men most detestable to be rehearsed."

[1] Cavendish, *op. cit.*, p. 224.

Wolsey answered him from his seat beneath a cloth of gold that " *Domine Doctor, magis reverenter.*" "'No, no,' quoth Ridley, 'there belongeth no reverence to be given to these abominable presumptions ; for an unreverent tale would be unreverently answered.' And there they left and proceeded no farther at that time."[1]

[1] Cavendish, *op. cit.,* p. 225.

CHAPTER XIV

THE HEARING OF EVIDENCE

CAMPEGGIO was guilty of an egregious blunder in admitting evidence, at that stage of the proceedings, to establish the nature of Arthur's marital relations with Catherine. He did not do his duty. He allowed himself to be swept off his feet by Wolsey, to be precipitated into taking a deplorable decision. Most authors accuse him of dilatoriness. But the unpardonable error he committed in this ruling is irrefutable proof that he went forward when he should have marked time.

In making this unequivocal statement we have not forgotten that we have said that this litigation did not envisage the dissolution of Henry's marriage with Catherine—that it was not a divorce suit. It was, we pointed out, an action which hinged upon the validity of the King's union to the Queen. It attacked the very existence of any matrimonial tie between them and thus did not fall within the purview of the maxim invoked by the Bishop of Rochester when he spoke of " what God hath joined together let no man rent asunder."

While all this is true, Catherine had produced a second Bull, the one that the prescience of her mother,

Isabella of Castille, had exacted of the Pope. As we have seen, it granted her and Henry a Dispensation to marry, even although Arthur may have had carnal knowledge of his wife.[1] We have already explained that Wolsey, recognizing that if this Breve was genuine his case was lost, had attacked its authenticity. He had, as we have said, adopted a procedure analogous to the modern French practice of an *inscription en faux*.

It is not an easy matter to explain all these niceties of a system of laws alien to English minds without going into details which are not only most technical but also extremely uninteresting. We shall, however, endeavour to drive home our meaning by an illustration based upon the codes now enforced in France. The point which we are discussing is so important that we cannot allow it to escape us.

Article 162 of the French Civil Code reads as follows :

" Marriage, in the collateral line, is prohibited between brothers and sisters, whether legitimate or natural and between in-laws (*alliés*) of the same degree."

Article 164 introduces that system of Dispensations dear to Canon and Civil Law. It sets forth that :

The King (now the President of the Republic) may, in specific cases and for grave reasons, do away with the inhibition decreed by Articles 162 and 163 in so far as they bear upon the marriage of in-laws.

We have before us, therefore, a rule of law now

[1] Burnet, Vol. I, p. 89.

applicable in France which fits our case like a glove. If a brother-in-law and a sister-in-law, a Henry and a Catherine, desire to marry in that country they must now obtain a Dispensation from the President of the Republic. The validity of their union thus depends upon the authenticity of this official document.

If, at a subsequent date, when the foresight of the man and the frugality of the woman will have filled their *bas de laine* with the best of securities, when death will have brought an end to their earthly happiness and when the greed of his relatives will have come into play, the validity of their marriage will turn upon the authenticity of this Presidential Dispensation, which the wife has hidden away with her gold.

Her production of that *pièce* will be met by an immediate *inscription en faux à son encontre*. We cannot translate these words because they are the very essence of all that is Latin in the civilization that is now French. They mean that the man's heirs will challenge the genuineness of this Dispensation by resorting to the *procédure d'inscription en faux* set forth in the French Code of Civil Procedure.

The result of this frontal attack upon this crucial exhibit is that it becomes the duty of the Court to refrain from passing judgment on the merits of the case proper until this ancillary matter—this *incident d'inscription en faux*—is disposed of. In a word, until the trial judge knows whether this Dispensation

is or not authentic it behoves him to mark time.
There are penalties prescribed for the resort to an
unsuccessful *inscription en faux*. This rule of
practice has features which are commendable and
which harmonize admirably with the entire spirit of
French institutions.

Let us get away from the Civil Law of the
twentieth century and delve once more into the
Canon Law of the sixteenth. The King's attack
upon the authenticity of the second Dispensation
was tantamount to the *inscription en faux* of these
ravenous French heirs. What Campeggio should
have done was to postpone the hearing of Henry's suit
until this ancillary question had received its solution.

If the Bull, which Isabella appears to have considered essential to her daughter's dignity, had been
recognized as being genuine—as being sincere as
the modern French would express it—there would
have been no reason for inquiring into these delicate
matters affecting the marital relations between
Arthur and Catherine. The sole issue before the
Legatine Court would then have been a clear cut
question of law—could the Pope validly grant a
Dispensation to override the prohibition set forth
in the oft-quoted Levitical text ?

We cannot exonerate Campeggio for his share
in writing this distressing chapter of history. He
was a Canonist. He knew his substantive and his
adjective law. He personified the judicial authority
of the Papacy. He committed the unforgivable
offence of allowing himself to be dragooned into

acting when, had he been worthy of his judicial ermine, he would have refused to be coerced into proceeding as long as the *incident d'inscription en faux*—the attack upon the second Dispensation— remained suspended in midair.

No crime is more reprehensible in a judge than that of moral cowardice, of bowing before expediency, of yielding to pressure. The penal code can, for malfeasance or nonfeasance, convert his wig and gown into the drab colours of a convict's garb. We fear that no penalty, other than obloquy, awaits him for yielding to intangible influences which capitalize his timidity but which cannot be established for certain.

We know that the inquiry into the genuineness of this second Dispensation could not readily have been carried on except at Rome. We have no difficulty in understanding that Henry would have been reluctant to have so important an issue tried out of England. But such considerations should not have forced Campeggio's hand.

The second Dispensation had been offered in evidence. If it were declared to be genuine parole testimony in regard to the intimate marital relations between Arthur and Catherine was irrelevant. No modern French judge would have gone into the merits of the case until the *incident d'inscription en faux* had been adjudged. Campeggio lost his head. He should have said to the King :

" Unless you withdraw your objections to the genuineness of this exhibit the trial cannot proceed."

The harassed judge took the line of least resistance. Henry and Wolsey, the Norfolks and Anne would brook no delay. He yielded to them and in doing so wrote his own epitaph. Not content with tarnishing his own escutcheon he played his part in besmirching the shield of some of the greatest families in English history. Let Herbert give us an insight into the testimony that Campeggio's opportunism wrote into the transcript we are now analysing :

The Life and Raigne of King Henry the Eighth thus introduces the subject to us :

" Businesses being thus ripe for examination of Witnesses, the Depositions of two ancient Ladies, who excus'd themselves by their infirmity from appearing in person were publikely read.

" (1) The first being Mary Countesse of Essex, said little, but in general terms."[1]

We should, perhaps, refrain from quoting the affidavit of the second witness because we have already referred to it. We consider, however, that it calls for repetition. It is thus handed down to us :

" (2) But Agnes the Old Dutchesse of Norfolke, who was present at the Marriage at St. Pauls in London, declared the age of Prince Arthur at the time of his said Marriage, to be about fifteen ; and moreover, did positively affirme, that she saw Prince Arthur, and the Lady Katherine, alone, in bed together, the next night after their Marriage. Which therefore, as also a following Deposition of

---

[1] Herbert, *op. cit.*, p. 242.

the Viscountesse Fitz-water, may serve to answer Sanders his tale, where hee saith, a grave Matron was put into the same bed with him, to hinder the Prince from knowing her Carnally."

The third witness bears a name which also stands high in the English peerage. Herbert's text reads :

" (3) George Earle of Shrewsbury depos'd, the Marriage was celebrated at St. Pauls, *Decimo septimo Henrici Septimi*, 1501, adding further, that Prince Arthur was born at Winchester, *secundo Henrici Septimi* and that he beleev'd the Prince knew his Lady carnally, both as being able so to do, as also because himselfe knew his Wife being not sixteen."[1]

William Warham, Archbishop of Canterbury, the prelate who submitted to the King the signature and seal which John Fisher, Bishop of Rochester, declared were forgeries, was the fourth witness. Sir William Thomas, Knight, followed him. Then came Sir Anthony Poynes, Knight, and after him Thomas Marquis of Dorset. The next in order was Robert Viscount Fitz-water. The only one of these five whose evidence is of any interest to us is the last. As we have already said a word about it we shall not again refer to it.

Thomas Lord Darcy, William Lord Montejoy and Henry Guldeford, Knight of the Garter, whose names appear under numbers 9, 10 and 11, " said little, but by way of publike report."[2]

---

[1] Herbert, *op. cit.*, p. 242.
[2] *Ibid.*, p. 243.

Charles Duke of Suffolk, Norfolk's co-leader of the Norfolk-Suffolk faction—was, in many ways, what we shall describe as the crudest of all the witnesses. As we interpret his evidence, he went so far as to declare that Catherine's robust sensuality killed Arthur. We may, perhaps, be mistaken in our deductions. We shall reproduce the text we now have before us. It reads :

" (12) Charles Duke of Suffolk deposed, that he was in the Bishop of London's Pallace, the morrow next following the day of Marriage, and that he waited there upon the Prince at Breakfast, confirming moreover in effect, the words of Maurice St. John, before set down. Furthermore, he added that the Shrovetide following the Marriage (which was in November preceding) the said Prince began to decay, and grow feeble in body ; which grew, as the said St. John related, by reason the said Prince lay with the Lady Katherine."[1]

Thomas Duke of Norfolke would not permit Charles Duke of Suffolk or Agnes the old Dutchesse of Norfolke to contest his right to rank among the leaders in this unsavoury competition. We have already heard what he had to say, but it may not be amiss to repeat his testimony so that it can be compared more readily with that of his coadjutors. Herbert's note about it reads :

" (14) Thomas Duke of Norfolke, Lord Treasurer of England, deposed, that he being the day of the Marriage in the Bishop of London's Palace, and the

---

[1] Herbert, *op. cit.*, p. 243.

THE HEARING OF EVIDENCE

morrow after, at the Prince's Breakfast, heard the Prince's words to Maurice St. John, when he said hee had been that night in the midst of Spain ; by which words, as also because Prince Arthur was a gentleman of a good Complexion, and nature, and above fifteen, he beleeves that he carnally knew his Lady ; because himself also at the same age did carnally know and use ; and he believes this the rather, that he heard from Credible persons, that the said Prince Arthur did lie with the said Ladie Katherine five or six nights afterwards."[1]

We shall now pass to the evidence of Thomas Viscount Rochefort. It is thus reproduced :

" (18) Thomas Viscount Rochefort, deposed, that hee heard divers of Prince Arthur's followers confirme the words he used, of his having been in Spain the night of his Marriage. Moreover, he heard say, that King Henry VIII, was persuaded by his Counsellor, about two yeares since, to abstain from the bed of the Lady Katherine, lest hee should offend his Conscience."[2]

The thirty-seventh witness brought the array to an end. She was Lady Elizabeth, wife to Viscount Fitz-water. She came to her husband's aid and the summary of her testimony reads :

" (37) The Lady Elizabeth, Wife to Viscount Fitz-water, depos'd that she saw the Lady Katherine and Prince Arthur in bed together, which was lest, and that she left them alone together."[3]

---

[1] Herbert, *op. cit.*, p. 244.
[2] *Ibid.*, p. 244.
[3] *Ibid.*, p. 245.

Burke's Peerage reveals no nobler names than those which we have just passed in review. The conclusion is thus driven home that we were not mistaken when we said that the best blood of England, or as Alexander Pope expressed it—" all the blood of all the Howards "—was behind the Norfolk faction in the effort to unhorse Wolsey, depose Catherine and seat Anne on the throne.

What is more striking is the proof that the women of the nobility vied with the men in this campaign. Those " two ancient Ladies," Mary Countesse of Essex and Agnes the old Dutchesse of Norfolke, would not have sent in these depositions when confined to their castles " by their infirmity," if they had not been deeply involved in the plot. Lady Elizabeth, Viscountess Fitz-water, would not have enacted the rôle of " last, but not least," if she had not had her heart in the fight.

The Catholic Church abhors scandal. Her experience across the centuries has taught her that :

" Vice is a monster of so frightful mien,
　As to be hated needs but to be seen ;
　But seen too oft, familiar with her face,
　We first endure, then pity, then embrace."

True to the principle compressed into these lines she recognizes that publicity acts as a sounding board to vice and that the flaunting of evil multiplie the effects of the wrong. Fisher of Rochester doe not strike us as being the erudite theologian tha his admirers would fain make him out to be. W

look upon him as merely " the holiest and wisest
of them."[1]   And by the term " wisest " we seek to
stress the element of common sense.

It was because he was the incarnation of rugged
honesty and discernment that he considered this
parade of distinguished witnesses a challenge to
fundamental morality.   Their recitals of the inner
details of the most intimate relations of life had gone
on for several days when his sense of propriety, his
horror of scandal, became so aroused that on June
28th, 1529, the monotony of the sittings was diversi-
fied by his intervention.   We shall allow Campeggio's report to Rome to tell us what took place.
He wrote :

" Yesterday the fifth audience was given ; that is
on 28th of June.   While the proceedings were
going on as usual, owing to the Queen's contumacy,
the Bishop of Rochester (Fisher) made his appearance
and said in an appropriate speech, that in a former
audience, he had heard the King's Majesty discuss
the cause and testify before all men that his only
desire was to have justice done, and relieve himself
of the scruple which he had on his conscience,
inviting both the judges and everybody else to throw
light on the investigation of the cause, because he
found his mind much troubled and perplexed."[2]

This excerpt from Campeggio's account of what
took place confirms the accuracy of Cavendish's
notes.   It shows that Fisher took Henry's statement

[1] Froude, *op. cit.*, p. 34.
[2] Brewer, *op. cit.*, Vol. II., p. 346,

O

seriously and that he believed that the King, like Goethe craved " more light, more light." It was for this reason that the Bishop of Rochester went on to say that :

" At the time of this offer and command of the King, he had forborne to come forward and manifest what he had discovered in the matter after two years of diligent study ; but now, to avoid the damnation of his soul, and to show himself not unfaithful to the King or neglectful of the duty which he owed to the truth, in a cause of such importance, he presented himself before their reverend Lordships to assert and demonstrate with cogent reasons that the marriage of the King and Queen could not be dissolved by any power, divine or human."[1]

Fisher was followed by Standish, Bishop of Saint Asaph, who covered the same ground. Another theologian imitated them. The Bishop of Rochester was not content with making this statement. He left with the Bench a written argument or Book elaborating his point of view. This attitude got on Henry's nerves and produced a torrent of royal indignation. It gave rise to a bitter reply, in the form of a speech in which the King attacked the character and conduct of Fisher with unsparing violence and acrimony. The arrogance of its tone, the biting sarcasm, the ill-concealed resentment all bespeak the depth of Henry's displeasure.

Fisher's protest failed to stem the current. The stream of witnesses remained unchecked. We have

---

[1] Brewer, *op. cit.*, Vol. II, p. 347.

already had before us a summary of their evidence. " Thus went this strange case forward from court-day to court-day."[1] On July 21st, 1529, the Court " sate to conclude the matter. . . . The King's counsel . . . closed their evidence, and summed up all that had been brought ; and in the King's name desired sentence might be given. But Campeggio . . . put it off till the 23rd being Friday ; and in the whole process he presided, both being the ancienter Cardinal and chiefly to shew equity. . . . On Friday there was a great appearance and a general expectation ; but, by a strange surprise, Campeggio adjourned the Court to the 1st of October, for which he pretended that they sate there as part of the Consistory of Rome and therefore must follow the rules of that Court."[2]

[1] Cavendish, *op. cit.*, p. 229.
[2] Burnet, *op. cit.*, Vol. I, p. 120.

CHAPTER XV

AVOCATION

WE have just seen that on July 21st, 1529, Henry's counsel closed their evidence, summed up the testimony, and, in the King's name, asked that judgment should be pronounced. Campeggio's refusal to comply with this request has brought upon his head the wrath of many writers. Froude informs us that he " acted on the Pope's last verbal instructions at their parting at Rome. He was told to go on to the last but that he must pause at the final extremity. He obeyed. . . . Wolsey declined to act without him, and Campeggio when pressed . . . answered ' Very well, I vote in favour of the marriage and the Queen. If my colleague agrees, well and good. If not there can be no sentence, for we must both agree.' "[1]

Let us admit, for the sake of argument, that Campeggio had received " verbal instructions " and that he " obeyed." It is reprehensible for a judge to obey. It is his duty to be guided by the dictates of his conscience and not to bend the knee, take hints or follow instructions. We have no abiding respect for Campeggio. We say this because he

---

[1] Froude, *op. cit.*, p. 107.

allowed himself to be browbeaten into admitting evidence that every gentlemanly instinct should have made him desire to exclude, if legally possible. But we are now dealing with a phase of the matter where these considerations cannot be permitted to warp our judgment.

The first thing that should be borne in mind is that Campeggio was not a judge in the strict sense of the term. The Legatine Court was not a Tribunal which had authority to render a decision. He and Wolsey were Commissioners delegated to hear evidence and report upon it. The Bench which they composed was a Board, rather than a Court. The Archbishop of York and all the Canonists of that epoch thoroughly understood this distinction. When Gardiner asked that Campeggio and Wolsey should pronounce judgment, he did not envisage an executory decree but merely a report.

The differentiation which we have just set forth explains, in a measure, Campeggio's attitude. It takes the sting out of Froude's charge that he had received " verbal instructions " and that he " obeyed." It does not, on the other hand, in any way exculpate him for having gone on with the trial, for having removed the veil of secrecy from the marital relations between Arthur and Catherine and for having authorized the unsavoury spectacle of the leading nobles of England vying with one another to show a remarkable lack of delicacy.

We shall not quote hoary texts of Canon Law or draw illustrations from the legislation of modern

France to support our statement. We shall look at the matter from the point of view of those fundamental principles of fair play dear to the heart of the Anglo-Saxon race. And in doing so we shall pay special attention to our facts. We shall not bother about law, whether it be canon, or civil or common.

We have not forgotten that when Knight, Casali, Fox and Gardiner were besieging Orvieto and asking that a Legatine Court should be appointed to inquire into the validity of Henry's marriage, the only Dispensation of which they had any knowledge was the one which Ferdinand of Aragon had obtained from the Pope. His daughter, Catherine, Arthur's widow, had informed him that she had been a wife in name only. He, accordingly, had asked for a Dispensation which was predicated upon that statement. He had obtained a Bull made out in accordance with his request. We do not go into the reasons which may have dictated his conduct. We confine ourselves to setting forth what he asked of the Pope and what he received.

This Dispensation, let us call it the " Ferdinand " Bull, gave rise to the question of fact which Wolsey sought to solve by having leading partisans of the Norfolk faction give the evidence which has been recapitulated in a previous chapter. Campeggio's ruling in admitting this testimony would have been perfectly proper if he had not known that after he had reached England Catherine had revealed the important fact that her mother, Isabella of Castille, more thoughtful of her interests and not such a schemer as her father, had had a second Dispensation granted which was in no sense predicated upon her having become a widow without ever having been a wife. This " Isabella " Bull admitted implicitly that Arthur and Catherine had consummated their marriage.

Wolsey did not know of this second Breve when he put his judicial batteries in place. Campeggio heard of it for the first time when he reached England. There is nothing to show that the attention of Clement VII had been called to it. It was only after the two Cardinals had been received in audience by Catherine that Henry became aware of its existence. She knew of it through her mother. We have already seen that Sir Francis Brian and Peter Vannes were hurried to Rome to find out all about it. Its existence was a surprise to the King and a bombshell to his Minister. We have not forgotten the desperate efforts that were made to keep it out of the record. It created a new issue that called for a solution.

If Campeggio failed to do his duty in admitting the evidence which was called for by the " Ferdinand " Dispensation without waiting until judgment had been passed upon the authenticity of the " Isabella " Bull and its falsity established, he had enough backbone left to refuse to submit his report until Rome had ruled upon the genuineness of this second Breve. Had he yielded to the pressure of the King's Counsel he would have aggravated the harm he had already done. There was, at that late hour, nothing for him to do, but to wait until the Holy See had expressed its opinion about the authenticity of the Bull which it was said that Isabella had obtained for her daughter.

Had Campeggio given in to Gardiner and submitted a report upon the evidence adduced before the Legates, he would have been forced to rule that Arthur and Catherine had consummated their marriage. The Queen had offered no testimony. She had confined herself to contesting the competence and the partiality of the two Commissioners. Such a decision would have turned out to be a gratuitous affront to Catherine had Rome subsequently ruled that the " Isabella " Dispensation was genuine. The recognition of the authenticity of this second Bull would have made it no concern of the Papacy whether Arthur had carnal knowledge of his wife or not. It would have narrowed the issue to a question of law and have made all verbal testimony irrelevant and impertinent.

Looking at the matter from this angle it appears to us that the criticisms levelled at Campeggio for having refused to do what the King's Counsel then demanded are based upon inadequate knowledge. He did the only thing that he could possibly have done at that juncture without making a mockery of fair play. No report could have been made until the Commissioners had been informed what had become of the attack upon the admissibility of the " Isabella " Dispensation.

Campeggio was a politician as well as a canonist. He foresaw that this " *inscription en faux*," by which Henry attacked the " Isabella " Dispensation, had changed the scene of action from Blackfriars to the Vatican. It is said that he reported to the Holy See " that if the King be cited to appear in person or by proxy, and his prerogative is interfered with, none of his subjects will tolerate the insult. If he were to appear in Italy it would be at the head of a formidable army. But if the avocation be merely intended to close my hands, and not to prevent the King from seeking a remedy elsewhere, it may be allowed to pass."[1]

Had the politician in Campeggio not gained the ascendancy over the canonist, he would have perceived that the consequences which might follow from Henry's appeal to ecclesiastical authority were no concern of his. The Catholic Church had not forced her jurisdiction upon the King. It was the " scrupulosity " of the royal conscience which had set in motion the entire procedure of Canon Law. Henry had literally imposed his worries upon the Papacy. If, to afford him the spiritual solace upon which he had so urgently insisted, it became necessary to carry on an inquiry at Rome, the political consequences of such an investigation were not factors which should have been considered by Campeggio.

The Pope looked at the matter in the same light as we do. Brewer, the liberal Protestant, calls

[1] Brewer, *op. cit.*, Vol. II, p. 357.

Clement " timid and irresolute."[1] Froude, the
spokesman of militant anti-Catholic sentiment,
describes him as " a weak mortal "[2] and repeatedly
impugns his sincerity and good faith. Pastor,
the distinguished exponent of Catholic scholarship,
in summing up his reign, says that " he was entirely
wanting in masterly initiative and courageous
decision."[3] It is said that Clement described the
predicament in which he found himself, when Henry
was pressing for judgment, as that of a man " placed
between the hammer and the anvil." It is added
that he bemoaned his hard fate and that weeping, he
prayed for death.

Clement VII has had no biographer.[4] The
historians of his time have passed severe judgments
upon him. There is " none so poor to do him
reverence." Catholic writers are not aware of it,
but their subconscious minds feel a distinct aversion
to the Pontiff who failed to stem the rising tide of
Lutheranism and during whose encumbency the
Church of Rome lost her crown's most resplendent
jewel. The result is that, to repeat his own words,
his reputation has been " placed between the hammer
and the anvil."

To our way of thinking, the very fact that, though
" wanting in masterly initiative and courageous
decision," he did his duty in the supreme tests to
which we have seen that he was submitted, demon-

---

[1] Brewer, *op. cit.*, Vol. II, p. 357.
[2] Froude, *op. cit.*, p. 100.
[3] Pastor, *op. cit.*, Vol. X, p. 331.
[4] *Ibid.*, p. 329.

strates that history has been unfair to him. We have followed his career through many phases of this most unfortunate case and we have not yet found an instance in which he did not face his responsibility.

Clement obviously was not one of those virile leaders who fairly revel in confronting difficulties and in riding roughshod over them. On the contrary, he was a timid soul, a prelate of a hesitant temperament, a man who suffered mental anguish and physical pain in coming to a decision. His was a nature to which the line of least resistance would have made a strong appeal. The fact that he bemoaned his hard fate and weeping, prayed for death and yet acted even as an English gentleman would have done under similar circumstances, impresses us as affording clearer proof of his inherent virtue than if, impervious to doubt, rising above fear, and delighting in a fight he had done the same thing in a more dramatic manner.

If we stop and consider Clement's physical appearance we have before us a key to his character. Pastor tells us that unlike most members of his house he was a good-looking man. " He was tall and had a graceful figure ; his features were regular and refined and only a close observer would have remarked that he had a slight squint in his right eye."[1] We suggest that that physical defect may have reacted upon his mentality, and made him timid. It may have given rise to what it is now more

---

[1] Pastor, *op. cit.*, Vol. IX, p. 247.

or less the fashion to call an inferiority complex. It may have caused him to be hesitant. We must not forget that he was a Medici and that the Florentine young man of those days did not have an Englishman's poise.

This squint did not in any way impair Clement's general appearance. " Only a close observer," Pastor tells us, " would have remarked " it. His subconscious mind, when put to the test, rose above this handicap, which he no doubt exaggerated. It nevertheless created that hesitancy of which we have spoken. It did not influence him when the crucial moment came. His better self, the good-looking man, and not the slight squint, then dominated the situation.

This lengthy excursion into the realm of conjecture brings us back to the hard and fast fact that during the summer recess of the Legatine Court the Pope " revoked " the cause, " avocated " it from Campeggio and Wolsey, " advocated " it to Rome and " issued letters citatory to the King and Queen to appear there in person or by proxy."[1]

We have just used three technical terms which mean that on July 19th, 1529, Clement VII gave instructions to his two Commissioners which were tantamount to saying that until the *Rota* had ruled upon the genuineness or spuriousness of the " Isabella " Dispensation, until the *procédure d'inscription en faux en cours* had ended, their mandate was suspended.

---

[1] Burnet, *op. cit.*, Vol. I, p. 122.

The revocation of the authority originally conferred upon Campeggio and Wolsey carried with it,
as a corollary, the advocation of the case to the
Papal Court. It was there that it was intended that
the inquiry into the validity of the second Breve
should take place. There was, perhaps, no legal
reason why this ancillary procedure should not
have gone on in England. There were, however,
difficulties of a purely practical nature that made this
almost impossible.

Moreover, Catherine had not only challenged the
competence of the Legates, but had questioned their
impartiality. We may say parenthetically that her
attack upon Wolsey's fairness strikes us as having
been a most serious objection. The advocation
of the case to Rome facilitated the holding of the
inquiry to which we have referred. It got around
the two exceptions filed by the Queen.

This advocation of the case created a stumbling-
block which annoyed the King. Logically there
was little or no difference between submitting on the
one hand (a) to the citation issued by Cardinals
Warham and Wolsey in May, 1527, and (b) to the
second summons sent out by Cardinals Campeggio
and Wolsey in June, 1528, and on the other respond-
ing to the process emanating from the Pope himself.
In all three instances the King was placed in a most
invidious position. It was his own fault, or, more
accurately, it was his " scrupulosity of conscience "
that had put him in such a position.

Logic has its limitations. The public opinion

that had countenanced the first two derogations from the royal prerogative would probably have baulked at the third.   In May, 1527, attention had not been centred upon the question.   The second feature had come to a head before its import had been appreciated.   By July, 1529, the situation had changed.   The meaning of the step would not then have passed unnoticed.   And besides Wolsey had told the King in 1527 and 1528 that these citations and summons were mere formalities.   Henry had learnt in 1529 that Clement was not a puppet controlled by the Archbishop of York.

When the Legatine Court adjourned, the King returned to Greenwich.   He there nursed his anger and took counsel with Norfolk and Suffolk and Anne.   Wolsey was not invited to participate in these deliberations.   He was not told that the days of his influence were over.   His Sovereign did not at once cease to employ him in delicate and difficult missions, but he was no longer Henry's confidant. Gardiner was installed as Chief Secretary and through his hands passed all correspondence addressed to the Prelate who had formerly been an omnipotent Minister.

Not content with conferring with Norfolk and Suffolk and Anne, and with relegating Wolsey to a more or less secondary position, Henry brought his favourite back to Court.   Burnet informs us that when he became reconciled to her, " as is ordinary after some intermission and disorder between lovers, his affection increasing, he was casting about for overtures how to compass what he earnestly desired. Sometimes he thought of procuring a new commission ; but that was not advisable, for after a long dependance it might end as the former had done. Then he thought of breaking off with the Pope ; but there was great danger in that, for besides that in his own persuasion, he adhered to all the most important parts of the Rome religion, his subjects were so addicted to it, that any such a change could not but seem full of hazard."[1]

As soon as Anne felt definitely assured of her return to the royal favour, she determined to unhorse Wolsey. Herbert attempts to make us believe that she and Catherine formed a working alliance to bring about his dismissal. The *Life and Raigne of Henry VIII* speaks of " the angry Queen and despighted Anne Bolen . . . who, though hating one another, did contribute to his destruction. The causes on the Queen's part," it adds, " are touch't before . . . and for those of Mistris Anne Bolen, besides her unkind Dismission from the Court (which conceiv'd to have been the Cardinall's advise) another inveterate grudge made her inreconcileable."[2]

We have often heard the expressions : " Politics make strange bedfellows " and " a fellow feeling makes us wondrous kind," but we cannot conceive of Catherine and Anne as allies even in sharpening a knife to decapitate Wolsey. We do not say that

---

[1] Burnet, *op. cit.*, Vol. I, p. 123.
[2] Herbert, *op. cit.*, p. 257.

he did not deserve any fate that they may have decided to mete out to him. We feel, however, that an impenetrable barrier separated them. We consider that the Cardinal's loss of Henry's favour can readily be accounted for without indulging in far-fetched surmises. He had played for high stakes and had lost. His dismissal from office was inevitable because Norfolk and Suffolk and Anne were not squeamish about precipitating him into the abyss that had long been yawning before his feet.

CHAPTER XVI

THE EPILOGUE BEGINS

CATHERINE misinterpreted the significance of the advocation of the case to Rome. She thought that it meant that the Pope would give judgment in her favour without delay. She overlooked the fact that inaction amply safeguarded her interests. It is true that the sword of Damocles still remained suspended over her head. With this single reservation, she was just as well off with the issue undecided as she would have been with a decree in her favour. She remained the King's consort.

Henry's reluctance to submit the issue to the *Rota* contrasted with Catherine's determination to obtain a judicial vindication. The entire aspect of the legal battle changed over night. A counter-offensive would have thrown the aggressor of the eve upon the defensive, had not the King held aloof from further action. It takes two contestants to bring about a battle. Henry simply and solely refrained from transferring his forces to Italy.

We now find Catherine urging the Pope, endeavouring to force him to pass judgment upon her demands. She held that her marital status had been challenged and that she was entitled to formal recognition of the validity of her marriage. The case, for a time, appeared to be no longer that of Henry *versus* Catherine, but of Catherine *versus* Clement.

We can well understand the Pope's attitude. He saw no prospect of bringing the King and the Queen together as long as the Norfolks had Henry's ear while Anne controlled the Monarch's heart and pandered to his passion. It followed that if a judgment had been rendered affirming the validity of the marriage it would not have affected Catherine's position one iota. There was, on the other hand, the imminent risk that Henry, if challenged, would carry out his threat and definitely break with the Catholic Church.

We saw, in our last chapter, that the author of *The History of the Reformation* tells us that even after the advocation of the case the King " in his own persuasion, adhered to all the most important parts of the Roman religion." The same writer goes even further and adds that Henry's " subjects were so addicted to it (the Catholic Church) that any . . . change could not but seem full of hazard." The Pope knowing of that principle boldly proclaimed by Luther, and of which we have already spoken, that a Chief of State had the right to prescribe the creed to which his nationals should adhere, found himself between the " hammer " of not acting upon the Queen's legitimate demand and the " anvil " of jeopardizing the spiritual welfare of those millions who were " addicted " to Catholic doctrines.

A strong ruler, full of self-confidence, would not have hesitated. He would either have inquired at once into the Queen's plea and have given a decision on its merits, or he would have ruled, without delay, that as the sole issue before him was one directly affecting the King's " scrupulosity " and only indirectly touching the validity of the marriage, Henry was at liberty to drop the matter, and that as no answer had been made to the citation it was assumed that the royal conscience was assuaged.

Clement was far too timid a man to have taken so firm an attitude. He preferred to mark time. He argued that " the Defender of the Faith," the student of the Bible who heard two masses a day and on Holy Days high mass as well, who had confessed his sins every day when the sweating sickness was raging in the summer of 1528 was beset by a fleeting temptation like so many other married men who have been the victim of a passing infatuation. He felt that Henry would soon tire of Anne and drift back to the Queen. He hesitated to challenge the Sovereign upon whose spiritual allegiance so much depended.

If we pause to consider the condition of the Catholic Church at that time we shall hesitate before condemning Clement for having been so circumspect. We do not contemplate reviewing the various matters which we stressed in the earlier pages of this volume and which bear upon the encroachments of Islam and the Schismatic Church in the East, of Lutheranism in the North and

Centre, of revolution in the South and of French apathy in the West.   What we have in mind is that when the problem which we are now considering confronted Clement, Catholicism did not have her batteries in shape to repel the assault.

Let us deal, in terms of men, with the point which has just been brought forward.   The Pope, during the first quarter of the sixteenth century, had under his command the intellectual resources of a secular clergy and of many religious orders such as the Augustinians, the Benedictines, the Carthusians, and the Carmelites.   We mean no disrespect to the high principled priests who made their influence felt in these various groups when we assert that whatever may have been their zeal and their scholarship, they were not equal to the emergency brought about by Luther's challenge and Henry's disaffection.

These prelates thought in terms of parchments and scrolls and manuscripts, not in those of printing presses and paper and multiple copies.   They were slow to adjust themselves to modern conditions and did not have the mobility of intellect called for by the new issues thrust upon a changing world.   They were not able to give the Pope that kind of support in launching a counter-offensive, called for by the intellectual needs of the hour.

We fear that a Pope of virile personality would have done far worse than did a timid man like Clement.   We recall that " Peter Vannes was commanded to tell the Pope . . . that if he did, for partial respects and fears, refuse the King's desires, he perceived it would not only alienate the King from him, but many other princes, his confederates, with their realms, would withdraw their devotion and obedience from the Holy See."[1] This was no idle threat. If the Pope had acted upon Catherine's insistence the King, led on by Norfolk and Suffolk and Anne, would have carried out this threat.

The result of Clement's timidity, of his refusal to allow the Queen to overpersuade him, was that when the break finally came between Rome and England, some years later,[2] the Jesuits had sprung into being. They were "printing-press" men, sons of the modern world and fully able to launch a counter-offensive. Any army that is condemned to remain upon the defensive is doomed to suffer eventual defeat. Ignatius Loyola, Xavier and Lainez and their adherents were not soldiers who locked themselves up in a fortress and complacently awaited the enemy. They went out and sought him.

Macaulay's immortal pages have recorded what their intellectual exploits made possible. The secular clergy and the other religious orders caught the contagious inspiration engendered by the Jesuits. Catholicism withstood the impact of the Secession of the English Church. If Catherine had had her way, if Clement had been a man of "masterly initiative and courageous decision," it might have

---

[1] Burnet, *op. cit.*, Vol. I, p. 94.
[2] Brewer writes : "Long down into the reign of Elizabeth . . . the old Faith still numbered a majority of adherents in England" (Vol. II, p. 469).

been reserved to an historian yet unborn to have written the lines to which we have just referred.

During the first months of Catherine's attempt to force Clement to act on her petition Norfolk and Suffolk and Anne were preparing to put the thumb-screws on Wolsey. They obviously effaced their own personalities and thrust that of Henry to the fore. He was a Tudor and loved the applause of the multitude. Or it may be that the King acted upon his own initiative. We have become so accustomed to looking upon him as a puppet made use of by others for their own designs that we may now be led into exaggeration. After all, the essential fact to be considered is that Parliament was summoned.

For many years Wolsey had governed England as he pleased. It was felt, either by Henry or by those who enjoyed his favour, that the time had come when there should be what President Roosevelt would call a " new deal." It was deemed expedient that the Cardinal should be compelled to render an account of his stewardship.

The Queen, who could think of nothing but her own wrongs, conceived the idea that the object of convening the two Houses was to launch a new attack against her. She requested the Pope to issue what was tantamount to an injunction, restraining Parliament from meddling with her.[1] We need not say that Clement refrained from taking any such foolish step.

[1] Froude, *op. cit.*, p. 110.

Parliament was brought together for other purposes. Immediately after recording this fact Froude's ardent patriotism causes him to write, in the selfsame paragraph, that

" Henry had no desire to break the unity of Christendom or to disturb the peace of his Kingdom for the sake of a pretty woman. The Duke of Norfolk, though he was Anne's uncle, if he did not oppose her intended elevation, did nothing to encourage it. Her father, Lord Wiltshire, had been against it from the start."[1]

We shall not attempt to gainsay what the author of *The Divorce of Catherine of Aragon* thus sets forth. We venture to observe, nevertheless, that it places the conduct of Wolsey's political enemies in a worse light than we would have thought of throwing upon our canvas. It tends to show that they used Anne for their own purposes and that they considered that she could be more valuable to them as the King's favourite than as his consort. It stresses the point that both she and Henry were political pawns used by designing men.

Be this as it may, the Parliament thus convened sealed Wolsey's doom. He sought to have posterity deal mercifully with him by passing this judgment upon himself : " If I had served God as diligently as I have done my King, He would not have given me over in my grey hairs. But this is the just reward I must receive, for in my diligent pains and studies to serve the King, I looked not to my duty

---

[1] Froude, *op. cit.*, p. 111.

towards God, but only to the gratification of the King's wishes."[1]

Wolsey was allowed to die in his bed without having his jugular vein severed. Ehses, the German historian, considers that his own words contain the epitaph that should be placed upon his tombstone. We cannot say that we entirely agree with so sweeping a verdict. It overlooks the Cardinal's ardent patriotism.

There was nothing of a " little Englander " about him. He had the vision of a statesman and the soul of a patriot. His overweening ambition inspired him to seek to humiliate Charles V, but the prestige of England at no time ceased to dominate his thoughts. Incorrigibly amoral, his treatment of Catherine was reprehensible. He sought to have Henry get rid of her so that an Anglo-French alliance could be brought about, which would strengthen the position of his country. We do not think that he would have descended to quite as low a level as did his political enemies, that he would have used a woman's body as a magnet and then have preferred to see her rule as a favourite rather than as a Queen.

When Wolsey was removed from the lists, the Duke of Norfolk became President of the Council, the Duke of Suffolk Vice-President, and Sir Thomas More, canonized in 1935, and now Saint Thomas More, Lord Chancellor. Pastor affirms that " after Wolsey's fall, Anne Boleyn, as the French

[1] *Historisches Jahrbuch*, 1888, p. 647.

Ambassador clearly pointed out, wielded through her uncle and father an influence in the Cabinet as unlimited as that which she had hitherto so long held over her suitor, the King."[1]   Froude, so often but not always, the antipodes of Pastor, records that " the King was thenceforth his own Minister. . . . He intended to rule, with Parliament to advise and to help him."[2]

It is not our business to ascertain whether Froude or Pastor accurately portrays the situation which followed Wolsey's eclipse.   Our thoughts must not be diverted from Henry's attack upon the validity of his marriage.   It is significant that no mention of the divorce was made in Parliament,[3] whether that body was dominated by the King, by Anne or by the Ministers of the Crown.

It was, however, common gossip in London that Henry did not intend to drop the subject.   It was said, in social circles, that by " English law females were excluded from the throne."   It was added that the King could not afford not to go on with the divorce as he had to have a legitimate male heir. So true was it that the matter was still uppermost in Henry's mind that about this time he wrote the Pope :

" We could have wished, not less for your sake than our own, that all things had been so expedited as corresponded to our expectation, not rashly conceived but according to your promise. . . . If

---

[1] Pastor, *op. cit.*, Vol. X, p. 273.
[2] Froude, *op. cit.*, p. 120.
[3] *Ibid.*, p. 123.

a Pope can relax Divine laws at his pleasure, surely he has as much power over human laws. . . . If your Holiness will keep the cause now advoked to Rome until it can be decided by impartial judges, and in an indifferent place, in a manner satisfactory to our scruples, we will forget what is past and repay kindness by kindness."[1]

This conciliatory attitude, which seemed to envisage a change of venue, does not appear to have pleased the Duke of Norfolk, for he told the Spanish Ambassador that "unless the Emperor would permit his master (Henry) to divorce the Queen and take another wife, there was no remedy left. The King's scruples of conscience (he said) instead of abating were on the increase, owing to the opinion of others who thought as he did."[2]

We thus see that whether the King ruled Parliament, as Froude asserts that he did, or whether Anne dominated the situation as Pastor would have us believe, the Norfolk faction showed no inclination to let Henry forget about his scruples of conscience.

The winter of 1529–1530 was devoted to collecting the opinion of the learned in regard to validity of the marriage.[3] Henry's delight at the favourable replies, many of which were obtained from French universities, was lessened by the fact that other institutions of equal repute declared that the dissolution of his marriage would not be justifiable

---

[1] Froude, *op. cit.*, p. 124.
[2] *Ibid.*, p. 128.
[3] *Ibid.*, p. 136.

unless it were shown that Arthur had had carnal knowledge of Catherine.[1]

The stress placed on this aspect neutralized, to a great extent, the favourable opinions which were submitted to the Holy See.   It soon became obvious that this form of pressure upon the Papacy would not produce the desired result.   Henry changed his tactics and on July 13th, 1530, had an address forwarded to Clement by representatives of the English clergy, nobility and gentry.

It was signed by the Archbishop of Canterbury, two Bishops, two Dukes, two Marquisses, thirteen Earls, two Viscounts, twenty-three Barons, twenty-two Abbots and eleven Commoners, " most of these," says Burnet, " being the King's servants." It was couched in these terms :

" The King's cause was now, in the opinion of the learned men, and universities both in England, France and Italy, found just, which ought to prevail so far with the Pope, that though none moved in it, and notwithstanding any contradiction, he ought to confirm their judgment ; especially it touching a King and Kingdom to whom he was much obliged. But since neither the justice of the cause, nor the King's most earnest desires had prevailed with him, they were all forced to complain of that strange usage of their King who both by his authority, and with his pen, had supported the Apostolic See and the Catholic faith and yet was now denied justice."

Passing   from   these   general   statements   the

[1] Pastor, *op. cit.*, Vol. X, p. 274.

signatories added that they apprehended great mischief and civil wars which could only be prevented by the King's marrying another wife, of whom he might have issue. The concluding lines of the address read :

" This could not be done till his present marriage was annulled. And if the Pope would still refuse to do this, they must conclude that they were abandoned by him and so seek for other remedies. This they most earnestly prayed him to prevent, since they did not desire to go to extremities till there was no more to be hoped for at his hands."[1]

Clement's answer was not delayed. Pastor characterizes it as " a calm refusal of this demand."[2] While we have no fault to find with this analysis, we think that it might not be amiss to have certain excerpts from this reply before us. They give us an insight into the manner in which the Pope proceeded. The document is written in the third person. Its opening sentence informs the various prelates, nobles and commoners that " he took notice of the vehemency of their letter, which he forgave them, imputing it to their great affection to their King."[3]

Clement then faced the two " grievous imputations " brought against him. He was charged with ingratitude and injustice. He submitted this answer to these attacks :

" He acknowledged all they wrote of the

---

[1] Burnet, *op. cit.*, Vol. I, p. 150.
[2] Pastor, *op. cit.*, Vol. X, p. 275.
[3] Burnet, *op. cit.*, Vol. I, p. 150.

obligations he owed to their King, which were far
greater than they called them, both on the Apostolic
See and himself in particular.   But in the King's
cause he had been so far from denying justice, that
he was often charged as having been too partial to him.
He had granted a Commission to two Legates to
hear it, rather out of favour, than in rigour of law ;
upon which the Queen had appealed : he had
delayed the admitting of it as long as was possible ;
but when he saw it could not be any longer denied
to be heard, it was brought before the consistory,
where all the Cardinals with one consent, found that
the appeal and an avocation of the cause, must be
granted."[1]

The pope then spoke of the opinions that had been
submitted by various universities.   He brought out
the fact that learned men were not of one mind
about this subject.   He then remarked : " He
must not precipitate a sentence in a cause of
such high importance, till all things were fully
heard and considered."   Here are his concluding
words :

" He wished their King might have male issue,
but he was not in God's stead to give it.   And for
their threatenings of seeking other remedies, they
were neither agreeable to their wisdom, nor to their
religion.   Therefore, he admonished them to abstain
from such counsels, but minded them that it is not
the physician's fault if the patient will do himself
hurt.   He knew that the King would never like such

1 Burnet, *op. cit.*, Vol. I, p. 151.

courses ; and though he had a just value for their intercession, yet he considered the King much more, to whom, as he had never denied anything that he could grant with his honour, so he was very desirous to examine this matter, and to put it to a speedy issue, and would do everything that he could without offending God."[1]

About this same time Henry's envoys appear to have importuned the Pope for the sanction of a double marriage. The same Sir Gregory Casali, who has already made a most unfavourable impression upon us,[2] seems to have been connected with this mission. He sent a report to London, dated September 18th, 1530, in which he sought to create the impression that the proposal had come from Clement and that it had been put forward by the Papacy as a solution of the entire difficulty. With characteristic effrontery he represents himself as having, " with an astonishing semblance of sanctimoniousness," replied that he dare not write in such terms to his Sovereign as he feared that the Royal conscience would not consent to such a solution.[3]

The only evidence adduced to show that this suggestion emanated from the Pope is Casali's word. It runs counter not only to common sense but to our knowledge of the Pope's excessive timidity. A contemporaneous dispatch forwarded to the King by another of his envoys, William Bennet, dated

---

[1] Burnet, *op. cit.*, Vol. I, p. 151.
[2] See Chapter VIII.
[3] *Historisches Jahrbuch,* 1892, p. 477.

October 27th, 1530, confirms our estimate of Casali's veracity.

It would seem that an attempt had been made to get the Pope to agree to a double marriage and that his hesitant nature gave Casali and Bennet an opportunity to importune him on this score. The matter recalls to our mind Tennyson's lines:

> " That a lie which is half a truth is ever the
>   blackest of lies ;
> That a lie which is all a lie may be met and
>   fought outright ;
> But a lie which is part a truth is a harder
>   matter to fight."

If we look up the history of Lutheranism and, in doing so, consult such a liberal Protestant authority as *The Encyclopædia Britannica*, we shall at once understand why it was that Clement permitted these English envoys to take up with him this question of a double marriage. We read in the standard work to which we have just referred :

" Recovering from his malady he (Philip, Landgrave of Hesse, 1504–1567) had returned to his intrigues when an event happened which materially affected the fortunes of the Reformation. His union with Christina was not a happy one, and having fixed his affections upon Margaret von der Saal, he obtained an opinion from Protestant theologians that bigamy was not forbidden by Holy Writ. Luther and Melancthon at length consented to the marriage, but stipulated that it should be kept secret. . . . The marriage, however, became known and a great outcry arose against Philip. . . . He objected to Luther's counsel to deny the existence of a second marriage . . . and caused bigamy to be publicly defended."[1]

With contemporary Protestant theologians, specialists in Biblical interpretation, thus holding in writing " that bigamy was not forbidden by Holy Writ," we can well understand why the timorous and conciliatory Clement did not refuse to listen to the ambassadors of the " Defender of the Faith " when they spoke of the advisability of a double marriage. It is most fortunate that we have Bennet's report before us. It shows that the Pope, however hesitant and vacillating he may have been, remained true to his past and at the decisive moment rose to the full height of his responsibility. Here are Bennet's words, as recorded by Pastor :

" I asked Clement VII, if it were certain that such a Dispensation was admissible, and he answered that it was not ; but he added that a distinguished theologian had told him that in his opinion the Pope might in this case dispense in order to avert a great evil ; he intended, however, to go into the matter more fully with his council. And indeed the Pope has just now informed me that his council (known as the Consistory of Cardinals) had declared to him plainly that such a Dispensation was not possible."[2]

This official report indubitably establishes that

---

[1] *Encyclopædia Britannica*, XIII Edition, *verbo* **Philip of Hesse,** Vol. XXI, p. 388C.
[2] **Pastor,** *op. cit.*, Vol. X., p. 276.

the Pope and his Consistory of Cardinals did not interpret Holy Writ in the same sense as did Luther and Melanchthon and the eminent Protestant theologians who, at approximately this same date, held that bigamy was permissible. Clement's hesitancy does him honour. The question which appears to us, with our twentieth-century conception of what is right and wrong, to be perfectly clear was not quite so obvious to the learned men of the sixteenth. We are not seeking to pillory Luther, Melanchthon and those who agreed with them. All that we hold is that the Pope was justified in investigating the subject and in keeping an open mind about it until he had before him the considered opinion of his official advisers. Fair play is our objective.

Q

CHAPTER XVII

PRÆMUNIRE

CLEMENT'S refusal to agree to a double marriage angered Henry. The Bennet report, which brought out that the Consistory of Cardinals had declared that such a Dispensation was impossible bears the date of October, 27th, 1530. There were no telegraphs or wireless or railways in those days. Means of communication were slow. The fact that on December 6th, 1530, the King wrote the Pope a letter containing violent complaints and taunting him with complete subserviency to the Emperor shows that he knew that this decision was irrevocable. When men lose their temper it is usually a sign that they recognize that they are in the wrong or that they have received a blow which staggers them.

Henry had foreseen that this unfavourable opinion would be rendered. We say this because Burnet informs us that on September 19th, 1530,

" the King, either seeing the Pope resolved to grant nothing, or apprehending that some bull might be brought into England in behalf of the Queen, or the disgraced Cardinal, did on the 19th September (1530) put forth a proclamation against any who purchased anything from Rome, or elsewhere, contrary to his royal prerogative and authority, or should publish or divulge any such thing, requiring them not to do it under the pains of incurring his indignation, imprisonment and other punishments on their persons."[1]

Henry followed up this proclamation by the publication of a lengthy dissertation defending his position and invoking arguments based on the Old and New Testaments, the authority of the Popes and Councils and the views of Greek and Latin Fathers and Canonists. He appears to have felt that so much learning should convince Catherine of the justice of his cause. He seems to have been surprised that she refused to yield to his demands. The nation began to take sides in the controversy. We are informed that " in the judgments that people passed the sexes were divided; the men generally approved the King's cause and the women favoured the Queen."[2]

The sixteenth century knew nothing of equal suffrage. Henry capitalized the influence he exercised over those who held the whip handle. He appealed first to the House of Lords, doing so on January 16th, 1531. Two months later the Lord Chancellor, Sir Thomas More, with twelve lords, spiritual and temporal, went down to the Commons and presented the royal case to them.

Catherine had no way of mobilizing the support of

---

[1] Burnet, *op. cit.*, Vol. I, p. 152.
[2] *Ibid.*, p. 166.

the women. Her influence was thus dissipated. The men rallied behind the King's banner and Parliament, reflecting their views, seemed to be satisfied that the marriage was unlawful.[1]

With the lines thus drawn between the men ensconced in power and the women relegated to the vocative, somebody thought of resuscitating certain dormant legislation of the Edwards and Richard II. These statutes made it an offence, known as *Præmunire* for the Pope to interfere, under any circumstances, in the internal affairs of England. "Wolsey," says Froude, "had forgotten their existence when he sought and accepted the position of Legate of the Holy See. Henry had forgotten them when he applied for a Legatine Commission to try his cause in London. The clergy, who claimed to be independent of the State . . . all had forgotten them. But the acts themselves were unrepealed, and survived as a monument of the spirit of a past generation."[2]

A Papal edict of March 7th, 1530, contained threats of ecclesiastical punishments and censures for Henry and any woman who should contract marriage with him while the case was still under consideration by the *Rota*. This ruling was interpreted by the King as a challenge. He prepared his measures to disarm the Pontiff's legionaries. To clip their claws was not enough. Their mouths had to be controlled by bit and bridle. A general Con-

[1] Burnet, *op. cit.*, Vol. I, p. 167.
[2] Froude, *op. cit.*, p. 147.

vocation of the English clergy, held in the middle of January, 1531, was " put formally in possession of a fact which had appeared on the first rumour of it incredible—that the whole body of the clergy lay under *Præmunire* for having recognized Cardinal Wolsey's Legation and the Papal Bull by which it was instituted."[1]

Looking back at the matter across the span of four centuries it seems monstrous to us that Henry, whose "scrupulosity of conscience " had caused him to appeal to the Pope and literally to force the Holy See to issue the Papal Bull now complained of, should have been permitted to make a weapon of these laws which he had violated. But, when men are in what is popularly known as a " jam " they are rarely punctilious about their selection of arms. The King was certainly in sore straits in January, 1531.

We say this because we have already seen that " the women favoured the Queen." We now have Froude's assurance that a section of the clergy, led by the Bishop of Rochester, an influential contingent of " great ladies," and a " party of nobles " unanimously censured the King.[2] Henry had no way of silencing the women and the great ladies. Neither Sovereigns nor slaves can hold them in leash. Clergymen are but men. They can be made to listen to reason or to feel the crack of a whip.

The only hope that the King had to take the sting out of the Pope's edict of March 7th, 1530, was to

[1] Froude, *op. cit.*, p. 158.
[2] *Ibid.*, p. 158.

put the fear of condign punishment not in the breast of those who are impervious to discipline but in the soul of priests who can be made to feel the lash. He could not engage in a battle royal against the Papacy with both these elements against him and expect to win. He had to break up their alliance or bend his neck. We do not say that we approve of what he did. All that we are endeavouring to do is to account for Henry's resort to a weapon which, to say the least, was very rusty.

He did not seek to convert it into a rapier or even into a sabre. He made of it a sledge-hammer. The rust upon it thus did not affect its usefulness. It really added to its effectiveness in that it not only knocked out those against whom it was applied but it also covered them with a coating of deep brown which has permanently darkened their reputation. Froude does not wrestle with metaphors when he describes how Henry silenced the English clergy. They, he writes, "were subjects of the Crown not of the Pope and to impress the fact upon their minds they learnt that legally their property was forfeited, that they would obtain their pardon only on payment of a fine of a hundred thousand pounds and on distinctly acknowledging the King as the Supreme Head of the Church of England."[1]

The same author adds that "it was in no idle vanity, no ambitious caprice that Henry VIII demanded the title which had been so much debated.

[1] Froude, *op. cit.*, p. 158.

It was as a practical assertion of the unity and independence of the realm."[1] This may be true, in the sense that it may have been the corollary that flowed from the King's primary premiss. His postulate in January, 1530 was not so much the affirmation of the principle that England was to have but one sovereign supreme within her own limits, as it was to facilitate the realization of his desire to put a diadem on Anne's brow.

We do not know who conceived this idea of separating the " black regiments "[2] from the women and great ladies of the realm. The data available to us do not inform us whether it was Henry or Norfolk or Suffolk or Wiltshire or Anne or who it was who evolved this plan. We are completely in the dark in regard to this detail. Whoever it was who hit upon it was a psychologist who understood how to win political battles. Our admiration for him or her or them who rose to such heights of party generalship is only equalled by our withering contempt for the men of the cloth who cowed before such a ferule.

We do not say that we are opposed, in principle, to the spirit of *Præmunire*. On the contrary, we applaud it most heartily. We believe in the American rule of absolute separation between Church and State. It gratifies our pride to read Cooley's footnote in his edition of Blackstone's *Commentaries on the Laws of England*, that the entire chapter on

---

[1] Froude, *op. cit.*, p. 159.
[2] *Ibid.*, p. 159.

Præmunire " is wholly inapplicable in the United States."[1]   What we mean is that many members of the clergy who had championed the cause of the Queen, who had led the women and an influential group of great ladies in their support of her, completely changed their attitude when their purse was touched.

Clauses were written into the new legislation which extended the scope of the old laws of the Edwards and Richard II, and which recognized the King as " Protector and Supreme Head of the Church and Clergy of England."   To this title was added the proviso " in so far as was agreeable to the law of Christ."   Such uncompromisingly honourable men and such fearless defenders of the right as they saw it as John Fisher, Bishop of Rochester, voted for the act as amended.   We thus insist that we in no sense assail either the spirit of *Præmunire* or this law of Henry VIII which revised it.   What we criticize is the King's inconsistency and the subsequent cowardly attitude of the clergy.

As soon as this new legislation was adopted those who had conceived it had the satisfaction of seeing what an incomparable weapon it placed in their hands.   This is said because the Convocation that had done the King's bidding and that had done nothing inherently wrong in doing so, hastened to pray him " to accept 100,000 L. in lieu of all punishments which they had incurred by going against

---

[1] *Commentaries on the Laws of England*, by Sir William Blackstone, Edited by Thomas M. Cooley, Chicago, Callaghan and Co., p. 103.

the statutes of provisors, and did promise for the future neither to make nor execute any constitution without the King's license."[1]

When Parliament adjourned Henry endeavoured to persuade the Queen to desist from her appeal. It is said that " he grew very melancholy, and used no sort of diversion, but was observed to be very pensive."[2] However sad he may have been, and however greatly he may have been immersed in his thoughts, it is not suggested that he called out to Anne : " Get thee to a nunnery, go." As long as his depression and reverie permitted him to seek solace in the embraces of another it does not surprise us to learn that Catherine met his entreaties with the reply " that she prayed God to send the King a quiet conscience but she was his lawful wife and would abide by it, till the Court of Rome declared the contrary."[3]

Such unshaken determination, aided and abetted, as the language of Old Bailey would express it, by the King's carnal concupiscence, the political generalship of the leaders of the Norfolk faction and Anne's " constant virginity " which had ripened into docility, caused Henry to refrain from seeing Catherine or to receive any tokens from her and provoked him " to send her word to choose where she had a mind to live, in any of his manors. She answered, that to which place soever she was removed 'nothing could remove her from being his

---

[1] Burnet, *op. cit.*, Vol. I, p. 177.
[2] *Ibid.*, p. 179.
[3] *Ibid.*, p. 179.

wife.' Upon this answer the King left her at Windsor, the 14 of July (1531) and saw her no more. She removed first to Moor, then to Easthampstead, and at last to Ampthill, where she stayed longer."[1]

This banishment of the Queen from the King's bed and board gave rise to a letter by Clement to Henry, dated January 25th, 1532. In it the Pope wrote:

" that he had heard reports which he very unwillingly believed that the King had put away his Queen, and kept one Anne about him as his wife ; which, as it gave much scandal, so it was a high contempt of the Apostolic See, to do such a thing while his suit was still depending, notwithstanding a prohibition to the contrary. Therefore, the Pope, remembering his former merits, which were now likely to be clouded with his present carriage, did exhort him to take home his queen, and to put Anne away ; and not to continue to provoke the Emperor and his brother by so high an indignity, nor to break the general peace of Christendom, which was its only security against the power of the Turk."[2]

This letter does not appear to have been delivered to Henry until May 13th, 1532.[3] Such a delay cannot be explained by the slowness of the means of communication. We are not able to account for it. All that we can say is that Burnet says that he has been unable to find any answer to it[4] and that Pastor

---

[1] Burnet, *op. cit.*, Vol. I, p. 180.
[2] *Ibid.*, p. 186.
[3] Pastor, *op. cit.*, Vol. X, p. 280.
[4] Burnet, *op. cit.*, Vol. I, p. 186.

affirms that it produced no effect.[1]   This silence, to
our mind, was equivalent to a reply.   It appears to
us to be all the more obvious because in the spring
of that year Henry and his board of strategy had
Parliament enact a measure abolishing annates but
left the execution of it to the King's discretion.

The milk in the coconut of this legislation was
compressed into the proviso making the application
of the statute dependent upon Henry's pleasure.
If we bear in mind how the clergy of England were
weaned away from the women and great ladies of
the land and how the overwhelming majority of the
prelates winced when the King announced that they
lay under *Præmunire*, we shall have no difficulty in
understanding the objective of the legislation we
are now considering.   We shall let Burnet guide
us in our investigation.   He writes :

" The substance of it is as follows :

" That great sums of money had been conveyed
out of the Kingdom, under the title of annates, or
first fruits to the Court of Rome, which they extorted
by restraint of bulls and other writs ; that it
happened often, by the frequent deaths of
archbishops and bishops to turn to the utter undoing
of their friends who had advanced these sums for
them.   These annates were founded on no law ;
for they had no other way of obliging the encumbents
of sees to pay them, but by restraining their bulls.
The Parliament, therefore, considering that these
were first begun to be paid to defend Christendom

---

[1] Pastor, *op. cit.*, p. 280.

against infidels, but were now turned to a duty claimed by that court against all right and conscience, and that vast sums were carried away upon that account, which from the second year of King Henry the Seventh to that present time amounted to eight hundred thousand ducats, besides many other heavy exactions of that court, did declare that the King was bound by his duty to Almighty God, as a good Christian Prince, to hinder these oppressions."[1]

There is cadence in the rhythm of this appeal to Henry's " scrupulosity." The figure, eight hundred thousand ducats, and the reference " to other heavy exactions," have a clarion note about them that recall a *crescendo* in modern orchestration. But the practical politics in this inspiring composition is found in this statement by the same writer, the author of *The History of the Reformation* :

" The Parliament, not willing to go to extremities, remitted the final ordering of that act to the King, that if the Pope would either charitably and reasonably put down the payment of annates, or so moderate them that they might be a tolerable burden, the King might, at any time before Easter, 1533, or before the next session of Parliament, declare by his letters patents, whether the premises or any part of them should be observed or not, which should give them the full force and authority of law."[2]

Nothing succeeds like success. We spoke in

---

[1] Burnet, *op. cit.*, Vol. I, p. 185.
[2] *Ibid.*, p. 185.

admiration of the political generalship that enabled
Henry's advisers to break up the alliance between a
segment of the English clergy on the one hand, and
the women and a body of the great ladies of England
on the other. We made it clear that we considered
that whoever it was evolved that plan understood
human psychology and capitalized this knowledge
in order to facilitate the execution of the King's
design. In resorting to the same tactics in this
attempt to coerce the Pope the same deft hands lost
their cunning.

If we pause for an instant we shall readily see
that the purpose envisaged by the authors of the
act abolishing annates was to put a club in the
hands of Henry and enable him to say to Clement ;
" Annul my marriage or rather ease my conscience
by declaring it invalid, and I shall allow you to
continue to collect annates. You and your pre-
decessors have amassed from this source since the
days of my father an aggregate sum of eight hundred
thousand ducats besides enjoying other perquisites.
If you do not do what I wish and if you do not do
so before Easter 1533 or before Parliament reconvenes,
this stream of gold will be automatically stopped."

Those who had seen how the English clergy had
knuckled under when the possibility of the King's
not continuing their pensions and other Church
preferments[1] was called to their attention and when
the menace of being forced to pay a heavy fine was
kept dangling before their eyes, imagined that the

[1] Burnet, *op. cit.*, Vol. I, p. 177.

Pope and his advisers would hasten to capitulate when this bait of gold was held out to them. They overlooked the fact that while Clement was not a strong man he had never yet faltered when put to the supreme test. Timorous and over-circumspect he was neither venal nor false.

Herbert brings out that " in this Statute the King and his Parliament declare that they doe not intend to use any extremity or violence before gentle and courteous wayes have been attempted." He adds : " This Act being pass'd, our King made use thereof, to terrifie the Pope, which also tooke effect, as I find by our Ambassadours Letters Dated from Rome April 29th 1532, though together (as they were instructed from hence) his Holinesse was told by them, that our King had reserved the whole businesse to his own power and Discretion, which however it appeas'd the Pope awhile, yet as matters past afterwards, the Statute had his finall confirmation. *Anno* 25. Henry VIII."[1]

The Pope's answer to what would be called attempted blackmail, if those who sought to apply so crude a form of duress did not occupy such exalted stations, was to order that a citation should be addressed to the King summoning him to appear at Rome in person or by proxy to answer the Queen's appeal. Henry did not reply with that boldness that we would expect of a Tudor and that would have characterized a Plantagenet. On the contrary, " Sir Edward Karne was sent to Rome with a

[1] Herbert, *op. cit.*, p. 331.

new character of Excusator. His instructions were
to take the best counsel for pleading an excuse of the
King's appearance at Rome. First, upon the grounds
that might be found in the canon law ; and these
not being sufficient, he was to insist on the prerogatives of the crown of England. Doctor Bonner
went with him, who had expressed much zeal in the
King's cause, though his great zeal was for
preferment, which by the most servile ways he
always courted."[1]

The fact that when it was seen that the Pope
would not yield to coercion an Excusator was sent
to the Papacy " to take the best counsel for pleading
an excuse of the King's appearance at Rome,"
nullifies, to our mind, the moral significance of that
law which revised the old statutes of *Præmunire*.
If the whole body of the priesthood " lay under
Præmunire for having recognized Cardinal Wolsey's
Legation and the Papal Bull by which it was
instituted,"[2] it strikes us that the mission of this
Excusator was equally illegal. We are thus fortified
in our belief that the intention of that statute was
not to lead up to the fact that the King was " the
Supreme Head of the Church and Clergy of England,
in so far as it was agreeable to the law of Christ,"
but that it was enacted in order to deprive the
women and a faction of the great ladies of England
of the co-operation of the priests in their
championing of Catherine's cause.

[1] Burnet, *op. cit.*, Vol. I, p. 188.
[2] Froude, *op. cit.*, p. 158.

Whether our theory be correct or not the fact stands out that even after Henry had had his spiritual authority officially proclaimed he continued to recognize the right of the Papacy to pass upon the validity of his marriage. This means that as late as 1532, the King's sole contention was not that the Pope had no jurisdiction but solely that this competence could not be exercised at Rome. And even in taking that position Henry appears to have fallen back upon " pleading an excuse."

CHAPTER XVIII

THE NEW ARCHBISHOP OF CANTERBURY

IT would be most interesting to know what Anne and, for that matter, Norfolk and Suffolk thought of Henry on April 30th, 1532. We refer to this particular date because on that day " one Temse, of the Lower House of Parliament . . . motion'd that they all should petition the King to take his Queen againe ; which being advertis'd to our King, He sent for Thomas Audley, the Speaker of the House, and told him . . . that it concern'd his Soule so much, that hee many times wish'd the Marriage had been good, but since the Doctors of the Universities had generally Declar'd it unlawfull, hee could Doe no lesse, than abstaine from her Company. Which therefore he wish'd them to take as the true reason, without imputing it to any wanton appetite : since, being in the 41st yeare of his age, it might be justly presum'd such motions were not so quick in him."[1]

Burnet's version of this statement to the Speaker differs in phraseology, but not in substance, from Herbert's report. It seems so strange to us to hear of a man claiming to be old at forty-one that we

---

[1] Herbert, *op. cit.*, p. 335.

prefer to have both texts before us. Here is the second one :

" It touched his soul ; he wished his marriage were good, but the doctors and learned men had determined it to be null and detestable ; and therefore he was obliged in conscience to abstain from her, which he assured them flowed from no lust or foolish appetite. He was then forty-one years old, and at that age those heats abate."[1]

We draw no deduction from the fact that Henry clamoured to be allowed to remarry so that he might have male issue while thus publicly insinuating that old age was beginning to take its toll of him. What we refer to is the stress placed upon his regret that his marriage was of doubtful legality. His language seems to imply that he ardently hoped that the Pope would ease his mind by declaring it valid. At all events, his words were not such as would be apt to please the designing politicians and the woman who was their lodestone.

This attitude of the King was all the more extraordinary because a few weeks earlier he had sent Sir Francis Brian to France to request the French Monarch to intercede in his behalf. True to his policy of resorting to coercion and of making use of threats Henry persuaded Francis to write Clement, on March 16th, 1532, that " the request of the King of England is just and he ought to relieve him or else they two (being *une mesme chose* and who have so well Deserv'd of him) shall be forc'd to seeke

[1] Burnet, *op. cit.*, Vol. I, p. 193.

such other Remedies, as shall not please him etc."[1]

To lend emphasis to this threatening language, Francis sent to Rome Gabriel de Grammont, Bishop of Tarbes and now a Cardinal, with instructions to drive home every point made in the letter. We may be certain that he executed his mandate with relish. He is the same prelate who had acted as Wolsey's tool in first injecting into the King's veins the virus of "scrupulosity of conscience."

Not content with thus invoking the aid of Francis and of making use of a man of Cardinal de Grammont's type in order to carry out his designs, Henry resorted to bribery in his attempt to get round Clement's conception of duty. When we make a statement of this character we prefer to have the author of *The History of the Reformation* speak for us. Here is what he writes under the sub-heading " The Cardinal of Ravenna corrupted by bribes " :

" He (the Cardinal) was at first very shy : at length he said, he had been oft deceived by many princes, who had made him great promises, but when their business was ended never thought of performing them ; therefore he would be sure ; and so drove a bargain, and got under Dr. Bennet's hand a promise, bearing that he, having powers from the King for that effect, dated the 29th of December last (1531) did promise the Cardinal for his help in the

---

[1] Herbert, *op. cit.*, p. 336.

King's affair, monasteries or other benefices in France to the value of six thousand ducats a year, and the first Bishoprick that fell vacant in England."[1]

The givers of bribes often throw away their money. Burnet appears to be anxious to demonstrate that Bennet was too prudent to squander Henry's ducats or to waste valuable sees. He thus hastens to add :

" This cardinal was the fittest to work secretly for the King, for he had appeared very visibly against him. I find also, by other letters, that both the Cardinals of Ancona and Monte (afterwards Pope Julius the Third) were prevailed with by arguments of the same nature, though I cannot find out what the bargains were."[2]

There is a note of sensationalism about this charge of corruption so categorically advanced against these three high dignitaries of the Catholic Church, one of whom subsequently became Pope. We are by no means convinced that the accusation is well founded. The only proof of the truth of this indictment available to us is the uncorroborated statement of the admitted corruptionist. Men who distribute tainted money have often been known to have an epidermis of a glutinous nature to which gold adheres. It is said that they do not specialize in telling the truth. It is conceded that their reports, while rarely supported by receipts, require corroborative evidence to give them any probative value.

---

[1] Burnet, *op. cit.*, Vol. I, p. 189.
[2] *Ibid.*, p. 189.

We do not say this in order to lead up to the point that certain Cardinals may not have had itching palms. There were, in those days, unquestionably corrupt men among them. All that we are endeavouring to bring out is that the unconfirmed statement of this Dr. Bennet cannot suffice to make out a case against those whom he accuses. It is, however, adequate to prove Henry's dereliction for the two obvious reasons : (1) that this document was found by Burnet in the English archives and (2) that it states specifically that Bennet was the bearer of " powers from the King to that effect dated December 29th last."

These desperate efforts to force the Pope's hand were made at this time because Norfolk and Suffolk and Anne were then becoming insistent and exigent. This is said because in the following September (1532) " the King created Anne Boleyn marchioness of Pembroke, to bring her by degrees up to the height for which he had designed her."[1] He had made his illegitimate son Duke of Richmond a few years earlier. There had been precedents for such honours paid to the adulterous offspring of royalty. We understand, however, that while many instances had occurred of great peerages falling to women, Anne was the first of her sex to be created a peeress.[2]

Such an epochmaking event called for great ceremony. Mille's *Catalogue of Honour* records that : " The King, attended by the dukes of Norfolk

---

[1] Burnet, *op. cit.*, Vol. I, p. 196.
[2] Strickland, *op. cit.*, Vol. II, p. 640.

and Suffolk, the French Ambassador and many peers, besides the Privy Council, went on Sunday 1st September, 1532, to the State apartment in Windsor castle. . . . To this room Anne Boleyn was conducted by a great train of courtiers and the nobility, both lords and ladies. First entered Garter, King-at-arms, bearing the King's patent of nobility. After Garter came the lady Mary, daughter to the Duke of Norfolk and cousin-german to Anne Boleyn, carrying on her left arm a robe of state, made of crimson velvet furred with ermine and in her right hand a coronet of gold. She was followed by Anne herself, with her hair loose hanging down her shoulders, attired in her inner garments, called a surcoat, of crimson velvet lined with ermine also, and with short sleeves ; she walked between Elizabeth Countess of Rutland and Dorothy Countess of Sussex, and she was followed by many noble gentlewomen.''

Further details of the ceremony are given but we shall not mention them. It is enough to say that the original patent of nobility granted Anne, which is still preserved in Chapter House, Westminster, gives her and her heirs after her, precedence over all other marchionesses.[1] The honour thus conferred upon her who had replaced Catherine in the King's affection and the scandal created by such ostentation did not pass unnoticed by Clement. He wrote Henry condemning such conduct.

We have just seen that the French Ambassador

---

[1] Strickland, *op. cit.*, Vol. II, p. 640 (note).

was present at Anne's investiture. Diplomatists
are the most circumspect of men. They never
make an advance without thinking of safeguarding
their retreat. We may be certain that the envoy
did not attend this ceremony without knowing that
his Monarch approved of his act. He may even
have had orders to do so for we read that:

" as for the matter of the King's divorce, Francis
encouraged him to go on in it, and in his intended
marriage with Anne Boleyn, promising, if it were
questioned, to assist him in it."[1] Led on by such
language, a few weeks later (October, 1532) Henry
had Anne accompany him to Calais. He there
presented her to Francis as his future Queen.[2]

We said a few moments ago that when Clement
learnt that the King had raised Anne to the peerage
he wrote a letter protesting against this action. We
have not been able to lay our hands upon it. We
know on the other hand, from Pastor's history that
when Henry took this trip to Calais " the Pope
threatened the adulterous couple with excommunication if they did not separate before the expiration of
a month and if Henry did not return to his legitimate
consort."[3]

We are inclined to believe that as the excursion
to Calais was in the nature of a honeymoon trip,
not following a wedding but in celebration of this
induction into the peerage, the Pope learnt of both
events at the same time and that he wrote but one

---

[1] Burnet, *op. cit.*, Vol. I, p. 196.
[2] Pastor, *op. cit.*, Vol. X, p. 280.
[3] *Ibid.*, p. 280.

letter. We have so far not found a specific instance in which Clement proved false to his trust. Our assumption thus falls entirely within the realm of probability.

Although we now have indubitable evidence that in September, 1532, Henry was preparing to bring Anne " by degrees up to the height for which he had designed her," Edward Karne, his emissary, or Excusator appeared before the *Rota* on November 14th, 1532, and " answered publiquely."[1]

Consistency is obviously not a jewel which found a place in the King's crown. Knowing, however, that Norfolk and Suffolk and Anne must have had Henry completely in their hands in the autumn of 1532, we are surprised to have the information driven home that when Edward Karne thus " answered publiquely " the Pope's citation he said that :

" the proceeding was undue, both as the question concerning his Excusation was not yet Decided, and that hee could not get a Copy of the Citation ; and finally it was not congruous to the Breve sent to the King concerning this businesse. Besides the Emperour was so powerfull in Rome that hee could not expect justice. Wherefore, unless they Desisted, he Declared, that, he must Appeale from thence to the able men in some indifferent Universities. And that, if this were refused, he protested then a Nullity in all that they did."[2]

---

[1] Herbert, *op. cit.*, p. 336.
[2] *Ibid.*, p. 336.

This dilatory exception did not assert that supreme authority of the King which Parliament had decreed. On the contrary, it brushed aside the recent legislation. It seemed to show that Henry was blowing hot one day and cold the next.

Henry's inconsistency brought out the fact that he was a weak man who did not know his own mind. He had apparently defied the Pope in September, 1532, when Anne was created Marchioness of Pembroke, but this plea, filed by Edward Karne ten weeks later, was in the nature of a recantation of that challenge. Clement may well have said to himself :

" I have before me an ill-mannered man in whom atavism and sexual desires are battling for control. By day his religious instincts gain the ascendancy but by night his lust runs amuck. This swing of the pendulum cannot go on indefinitely. Sooner or later it will veer definitely either to the right or the left. It is my duty, as the Head of the Catholic Church, to do nothing which will prevent him from returning to his old moorings. In fact, I owe it to the millions of Englishmen who will be affected by his decision to do my utmost to keep ajar the door of hope."

When the Pope was thus making every endeavour to propitiate the King, while never failing to remonstrate with him at every new overt act, Henry was becoming more and more infatuated with Anne— or perhaps she was becoming more and more exigent. This is obviously a detail which our researches do not permit us to elucidate. All that they reveal to us is that when this pre-nuptial honeymoon trip to France had served its purpose, Henry and Anne returned to Calais, "yet as the weather was then tempestuous, hee passed not the Seas before the 14th of November ; on which day some write, He privately marryed the Marchionesse, though others place it on the 25th of January following, Rowaland Lee, afterwards Bishop of Coventry and Lichfield, and President of Wales . . . celebrating the Marriage in the presence of Arch-Bishop Cranmer, the Duke of Norfolke, and her Father, Mother and Brothers, etc, which yet was not published till Easter following."[1]

Here is how Burnet makes this same announcement :

" He (Henry) married Anne Boleyn on the 14th of November (1532), on his landing in England, but Stow says it was on the 25th of January 1533. . . . The grounds on which the King did this were, that his former marriage being of itself null, there was no need of a declarative sentence after so many universities had given their judgments against it. Soon after the marriage she was with child, which was looked on as a signal evidence of her chastity, and that she had till then kept the King at a due distance."[2]

Strickland thus sums up this question of the date of Henry's marriage :

" The time and place of Anne Boleyn's marriage with

---

[1] Herbert, *op. cit.*, p. 340.
[2] Burnet, *op. cit.*, Vol. I, p. 198.

Henry VIII are disputed points in history.   Some authors have affirmed that she was privately united to the King at Dover the same day they returned from France, being the festival of St. Erkenwald ; according to others the nuptials were secretly performed in the presence of the Earl and Countess of Wiltshire, and the Duke and Duchesse of Norfolk in the chapel of Sopewell nunnery. . . . The unpopularity of this union was the cause of the profound secrecy with which the nuptials between Henry and his fair subject were solemnized ; for the same reason it was necessary to keep the matter from the public as long as it was possible to do so.''[1]

The unfortunate feature of this uncertainty about the date of the marriage is that Queen Elizabeth was born on September 7th, 1533.   It is true that we have already seen that Burnet, who is a partisan of the 14th of November school, found in the fact that '' soon after marriage she (Anne) was with child'' '' signal evidence of her chastity,'' but the editor of his works has added this footnote :

'' Stow (an advocate of the 25th of January dating) is in the right ; for in a letter of Cranmer's to Hawkins, then the King's Ambassador with the Emperor, dated in June from Croydon, he wrote : ' Queen Anne was married much about St. Paul's Day last : as the condition thereof doth well appear, by reason she is now somewhat big with child.' ''[2]

It was not until April 12th, 1533 (Easter), that

---

[1] Strickland, Vol. II, p. 649.
[2] Burnet, *op. cit.*, Vol. I, p. 198 (note).

Anne appeared publicly for the first time as Henry's consort.[1] We are inclined to think that it was Cranmer who insisted that the moment had come to do away with this secrecy about the King's marriage.

He had long been what modern writers would call a pro-divorce man. As early as 1527 he had acted as one of the confidential advisers of the Norfolk faction.[2] It is said that he had been Anne's tutor.[3] When Warham, Archbishop of Canterbury, died in August, 1532, he was appointed to fill this important vacancy. He was in Germany when the honour was tendered him. He appears to have been reluctant to accept it. The choice was not agreeable to the English clergy, but we are told that " the King persisted in his opinion and the others were forced to yield."[4]

It is our belief that Cranmer owed this signal distinction to the triumvirate of Norfolk and Suffolk and Anne rather than to Henry. It was of paramount importance to these allies that the strategic see of Canterbury should be administered by a man on whom they could depend. Warham had played into their hands. He had been named as one of the counsellors to assist Catherine " but fearing to incur the King's displeasure and using his favourite phrase, *ira principis mors est* had given her very little help."[5] They needed, nevertheless,

---

[1] Pastor, *op. cit.*, Vol. X, p. 281.
[2] Brewer, *op. cit.*, Vol. II, p. 223.
[3] We find this statement in the index to Brewer's *Reign of Henry VIII* but the page referred to does not bear out this assertion.
[4] Burnet, *op. cit.*, Vol. I, p. 201.
[5] *Encyclopædia Britannica*, XIII Edition, *verbo* Warham William, Vol. XXVIII, p. 325 D.

a more aggressive champion than a weary octogenarian. Cranmer had the resiliency of mind necessary for their purposes. He was a "learned, prudent and resolute man."[1]

This designation of the new Archbishop of Canterbury affords another example of Henry's inconsistency and of Clement's spirit of conciliation. The King applied to the Pope to confirm the selection of Cranmer and to issue the necessary Bull. This request was honoured, and by a Papal Breve, dated February 22nd, 1533, Cranmer "was ordained to be consecrated." Burnet, who gives us this information, adds that he took "the oath that was in the pontifical."[2]

This latter statement is both accurate and, at the same time, misleading. If we turn to the *Encyclopædia Britannica* we learn that :

"It was the custom of the Archbishop elect to take two oaths, the first of episcopal allegiance to the Pope, and the second in recognition of the royal supremacy. The latter was so wide in its scope that it might fairly be held to supersede the former, in so far as the two were inconsistent. Cranmer, however, was not satisfied with this. He had a special protest recorded, in which he formally declared that he swore allegiance to the Pope only in so far as that was consistent with his supreme duty to the King."[3]

This same authority adds that " the morality of

---

[1] Burnet, *op. cit.*, Vol. I, p. 201.
[2] *Ibid.*, p. 202.
[3] *Encyclopædia Britannica*, XIII Edition, *verbo* Cranmer Thomas, Vol. VII, p. 375 D. See also Burnet, *op. cit.*, Vol. I, p. 202.

this course has been much canvassed, though it seems really to involve nothing more than an express declaration of what the two oaths implied."

Looking at the matter from the standard of the canons of Anglo-Saxon fair play, it appears to us that the fact that Clement was not apprised of this " special protest " means that the consecration of the first primate in the history of the Reformation of the Church of England was obtained under pretences which do no honour to Henry's name but which leave no stain on Clement's memory.

The agile brain which conceived the idea of the mental reservation " by which . . . he (Cranmer) did not wholly save his integrity "[1] was quick to perceive that Henry's marriage to Catherine could not be allowed to remain unannulled. As soon as the new Archbishop was consecrated he took his seat in the Upper House of Convocation. He there set in motion the judicial procedure called for by Anne's equivocal position and by the higher politics of Norfolk and Suffolk.

[1] Burnet, *op. cit.*, Vol. I, p. 203.

CHAPTER XIX

ANNE BOLEYN CROWNED

WHEN the Upper House of Convocation began its deliberations there were " hot and earnest debates upon these two questions :—Whether it was against the law of God, and indispensable by the Pope, for a man to marry his brother's wife, he being dead without issue, but having consummated the marriage and whether Prince Arthur had consummated the marriage."[1]

The Lower House voted, fourteen in favour of the affirmative and seven for the negative. But it was in the Upper Chamber that the full dress debate was staged. " The opinions of nineteen universities were read for it, and the one house being as full as the other was empty, two hundred and sixteen present either in person or by proxy, it was carried in the affirmative, *nemine contradicente ;* those few of the Queen's party that were there it seems going out. For the other question, about the matter of fact, it was remitted to the faculty of canon law . . . whether the presumptions were violent and such as in the course of law must be looked on as good evidences of a thing that was secret and was not

---

[1] Burnet, *op. cit.*, Vol. I, p. 203.

capable of formal proof. They all, except five or six, were for the affirmative."[1]

We need not be told that in the debate which preceded these tests of strength John Fisher, Bishop of Rochester, spoke against the motion. As far as we know Stokesly, Bishop of London, was the only prelate who supported him in the discussion. It was probably because their hearts were overflowing with sadness that they were not present when the formal vote was taken.

When this decision had been given, nothing remained for the Convocation to do but to give judgment and declare Henry's marriage with Catherine null. "The thing was already determined," asserts Burnet, "only the formality of a sentence declarative was wanting."[2] Norfolk and Suffolk, acting this time without Anne, had too abiding a respect for forms and precedents to give effect to this pre-ordained decision without recalling Catherine's existence. We are thus told that :

"before they proceeded to that, a new message was sent to the Queen, to lay all that had passed before her, and to desire her to acquiesce in the opinions of so many universities and learned men."[3] It is not necessary to say that "she still persisted in her resolution to own her marriage and to adhere to her appeal, till the Pope should judge it." She was a proud woman "and when it was told her that the King would settle the jointure that she was

---

[1] Burnet, *op. cit.*, Vol. I, p. 203.
[2] *Ibid.*, p. 205.
[3] *Ibid.*, p. 205.

to have by his brother, and that the honour of Princess of Wales would still be paid her, she rejected it."

The proof is thus more than manifest that though Cranmer, the new Archbishop of Canterbury and, we think, the canonical brains of the Norfolk faction, was a " learned, prudent and resolute man "[1] he presided at the ceremony which joined Henry and Anne in wedlock before he had carried out the formality of annulling the marriage which had declared Henry to be Catherine's husband. This irregularity might have escaped a " resolute " man but it would not have failed to arrest the attention of a canonist who was also " learned and prudent." If Cranmer thus subordinated his wisdom and his prudence to his resolution it is because circumstances compelled him to do so.

Let us permit the author of *The History of the Reformation* to enlighten us on this point. After having told us that Catherine peremptorily rejected the honours due a Princess of Wales, he goes on to say, in the very next sentence, that :

" the new Queen was now with child, and brought forth Queen Elizabeth the 7th of September this year (1533) ; from which, looking backwards nine months, to the beginning of December, it shows that she must have married at or before that time : for all the writers of both sides agree that she was married before she conceived with child. The

[1] Burnet, *op. cit.*, Vol. I, p. 201.

S

King, therefore, thought not fit to conceal it much longer ; so on Easter eve she was declared Queen of England.''[1]

The French, with their deft way of saying things, often remark when a viable child is born within less than one hundred and eighty days after the date of the marriage of its parents, *" Qu'ils ont fait leurs Paques avant Carême "*—that " they have celebrated Easter before observing Lent."[2] We do not suggest that the fact that Henry waited until Easter eve to announce his marriage had anything to do with the origin of this aphorism. Partisanship at one time ran so high in connection with all matters bearing upon Henry's divorce that this is not entirely impossible, even though Burnet's explanation may demonstrate that the remark would not apply to the birth of one of the greatest sovereigns known to modern history.

Had Henry not been a man of a vacillating temperament, a weak man, he would not have allowed so important a matter as the date of his marriage with Anne to be open to discussion. Gentlemen attach importance to such questions. The chivalrous instinct which is latent in them prompts them to do so. This entire problem is so complicated that we prefer to have Burnet explain to us, in his own words, why it was that the second marriage was

[1] Burnet, *op. cit.*, Vol. I, p. 205.
[2] We have referred to 180 days instead of the customary 9 months because Art. 314 of the French Civil Code says, in substance, that the child capable of living, which is born before the 180th day after the marriage, is not presumed to be the child of the husband.

celebrated so many months before the first was declared null. He writes :

" It seems it was not thought needful at that time to proceed to any further sentence about the former marriage ; otherwise I cannot see what made it be so long delayed, since the thing was in their power now, as well as after. And it was certainly a preposterous method to judge the first marriage null after the second was published. So that it seems more probable that they did not intend any sentence at all, till afterwards, perhaps upon advertisements from beyond sea, they went on to a formal process."[1]

By no means satisfied that this explanation would pass muster, this same historian feels called upon to put the blame on Clement. This he does by suggesting :

" Nor is it unlikely that the King remembering the old advice that the Pope sent him once to marry a second wife and then to send for a Commission to try the matter which the Pope was willing to confirm . . . resolved to follow this method."[2] It seems far more probable that Henry had married Anne, when he was still the husband of Catherine, because Cranmer had persuaded him to adhere to the school led by Luther and Melanchthon and followed by the German Protestant theologians, who held that bigamy was not forbidden by Holy Writ.[3]

---

[1] Burnet, *op. cit.*, Vol. I, p. 205.
[2] *Ibid.*, p. 206.
[3] *Encyclopædia Britannica*, XIII Edition, *verbo* Philip of Hesse, Vol. XXI, p. 388 C.

S*

This theory is made quite plausible when we recall not only Cranmer's high rank in the good graces of Norfolk and Suffolk and Anne, but also the fact that he had so many acquaintances in Germany, where he hid his wife during those days when priests were not allowed to marry. It is Herbert who thus gives us this information :

" hee (Cranmer) being a married man, through fearing of this law, sent away his wife for the present into Germany, she being kinswoman to Hosiander, the Divine of Noremberg, whom he married during his Ambassade with the Emperor about Anno 1532."[1]

It appears to us that the Archbishop of Canterbury convinced Henry that, as bigamy was permissible, it would be wiser to proceed with this second marriage without provoking the publicity necessary for the annulment of the first. The King, persuaded by this reasoning, followed Cranmer's advice, but, being of an unstable character, soon changed his mind and created the ludicrous situation to which we have already referred.

" Whatsoever were the reasons of this delay," writes the author from whom we have repeatedly quoted in this chapter, " the process was framed in this method. First Cranmer wrote to the King that the world had long been scandalized with his marriage, and that it lay on him as his duty to see it tried and determined : therefore craved he his royal leave to proceed in it."[2]

---

[1] Herbert, *op. cit.*, p. 448.
[2] Burnet, *op. cit.*, Vol. I, p. 206.

This authorization was granted. " Both the King and Queen were cited to appear before the Archbishop at Dunstable, the 20th May (1533), and the Archbishop went thither with the Bishop of London, Winchester (Gardiner), Bath and Wells and Lincoln and many divines and canonists." . . .

" On the 10th of May the Archbishop sate in court and the King appeared by proxy, but the Queen appeared not. Upon which she was declared *contumax*, and a second citation was issued and after that a third : but she intended not to appear, and so she was finally declared *contumax*.

" Then the evidences that had been brought before the Legates, of the consummation of the marriage with Prince Arthur were read. After that the determinations of the Universities and divines and canonists were also produced and read. Then the judgments of the convocations of both provinces were also read, with many other instruments, and the whole merits of the cause were opened. Upon which, after many sessions, on the 23rd of May (1533) sentence was given, with the advice of all that were there present, declaring it only to have been a marriage *de facto*, but not *de jure*, pronouncing it null from the beginning."[1]

It is naturally assumed that whatever criticisms may be made against a " process framed in this method " the whole procedure was carried out by an English ecclesiastical court which, eschewing and disdaining all connection with Rome, symbolized

---

[1] Burnet, *op. cit.*, Vol. I, p. 206.

the independence of the English Church and the autonomy of her hierarchy. This assumption appears to us to be self-evident. We find, however, that so consistently was Henry inconsistent, so constant was he in his inconstancy, so incorrigible was he in his fickleness, that the " Archbishop in the sentence is called the Legate of the Apostolic See."[1] This designation so shocks Burnet that he remarks that " whether this went of course as one of his titles, or was put in to make the sentence firmer, the reader may judge."[2]

If it was on Easter eve, 1533, that Anne was declared Queen of England, it was not until June 1st of that year that she was crowned. Herbert permits us to know just what Clement did when this information reached him. *The Life and Raigne of Henry VIII* contains this paragraph :

" And now the Newes of the Arch-Bishop of Canterburies Sentence, and open Marriage of Mistris Anne Bolen being come to the Popes eares and together with it an information concerning the Booke our King had compos'd against the Popes Authority (which also more than anything else offended him) the whole College of Cardinalls, especially such as were for the Emperour, became humble suppliants to the Pope, that hee would proceed rigorously against our King ; which also the Pope accorded though not in that peremptory and publique manner as was afterwards done."[3]

[1] Burnet, *op. cit.*, Vol. I, p. 207.
[2] *Ibid.*, p. 207.
[3] Herbert, *op. cit.*, p. 357.

We see from this that Clement acted when advised of Henry's marriage, but knowing that he was dealing with a weak man, who was the "Defender of the Faith" and whom he thought would in all likelihood repent sooner or later, preferred to refrain from anathematizing him. Here is how Herbert expresses this same thought :

" I find that this Sentence was not definitive in the principall cause but only declarative in the point of Attemptats (as they call it) in that King Henry (the cause yet defending) had Divorced Himselfe without the leave and authority of the Pope. Therefore it was declar'd that all his Actions herein were subject to a Nullity, and Himself to Excommunication, unlesse Hee restored things *in integrum*, for which time was allowed him, till the end of September following."[1]

From the Catholic point of view this second marriage was not merely null and void but non-existent. The situation created by it gave publicity and added affront to Henry's adultery, but it did not change the status existing before this formality was introduced. There was, therefore, on canonical grounds, no occasion for a renewal of the remonstrances already made. We could well have understood Clement's attitude had he ignored what he considered a travesty of marriage.

The Pope did not take any such detached view of the situation. Pastor tells us that on being informed of these proceedings he " hesitated in

[1] Herbert, *op. cit.*, p. 358.

characteristic fashion for some time, and then, at last, on July 11th, 1533 he gave sentence against Henry, pronounced the marriage with Anne Boleyn null and void . . . and laid the King under the greater excommunication."[1]

With these dates before us we are unable to understand what the brilliant Catholic scholar means when he says that before taking action the Pope "hesitated in characteristic fashion for some time."[2] Pastor appears to have overlooked the slowness of communications in the sixteenth century. He is so obsessed with the idea that Clement was a temporizer by nature[3] that, even when a confrontation of dates reveals that there could not have been any procrastination or tergiversation, we find that stubborn fact brushed aside as if it were an excrescence which well-mannered men are not expected to observe.

The session of Parliament which began in January, 1534, witnessed the enactment of a series of laws of an anti-Papal tendency. One of these contained a declaration against the " usurped authority of the Bishop of Rome," as the Pope henceforward was to be designated. By the Act of Royal Succession

---

[1] Pastor, *op. cit.*, Vol. X, p. 282.

[2] The exact date of Henry's marriage to Anne is a matter of conjecture (see page 257). The marriage of Henry and Catherine was annulled by Cranmer on May 23, 1533. We do not know when this decision was publicly announced or when knowledge of it reached Clement. Anne was crowned on June 1st, 1533. Assuming that the Pope was apprised at once of this coronation it obviously took some time for the news to reach Rome. Clement could not have been expected to act in so important a matter without consulting his advisers. His decree of excommunication is dated July 11th, 1533.

[3] Pastor, *op. cit.*, Vol. X, p. 331.

Henry's marriage with Catherine was declared null from the beginning and Princess Mary illegitimate. It was decreed, on the other hand, that Anne's children, and they alone, were in rightful succession to the throne. There then began what certain historians, indulging in undue emphasis, call a reign of terror.

While the official pendulum was thus swinging strongly toward the left, Henry, with that fickleness which seems to have been ingrained in his very nature, was working underground to have Clement annul his marriage with Catherine. This statement is most challenging. In order to test its accuracy we must watch not only our facts but our dates.

We rely in the main for this information upon Burnet's oft-quoted work. In this instance he does not furnish us with the dates which interest our narrative. He quotes, however, as his authority a letter published by Herbert and written to the King by the Archbishop of York and the Bishop of Duresme. It is dated May 11th, 1534.[1] When we refer to *The Life and Raigne of Henry VIII* we find this document set forth in full in its proper chronological order under the marginal heading " 1534," following incidents similarly designated as having taken place on April 17th, 1534, and preceding others mentioned under the date of May 20th, 1534.[2]

We stress this detail because Burnet records his statement under a 1533 date line, although all his

---

[1] Burnet, *op. cit.*, Vol. I, p. 213.
[2] Herbert, *op. cit.*, p. 374.

facts, when analysed, obviously refer to 1534, just as does his specific mention of this crucial letter dated May 11th, 1534. He begins by saying that the Bishop of Paris " prevailed with the King to submit the whole matter to the Pope and the Consistory . . . but the King, it seems, would not abase himself so far as to send any submission in writing, till he had fuller assurances."[1]

We shall not stop and inquire what these words " fuller assurances " really mean. We are inclined to believe that we grasp their import but we shall refrain from expressing an opinion. We are recording facts, not indulging in conjectures. We shall not even ask ourselves what distinction an English gentleman of to-day would draw between a verbal submission and a " submission in writing." We prefer to overlook such trifles and allow Burnet to resume his narrative.

It seems that matters went so far that " when the Bishop of Paris came to Rome, the motion was liked ; and it was promised, that if the King sent a promise of that under his hand, with an order to his proxies to appear in Court, there should be judges sent to Cambray to form the process, and then the matter should be determined for him at Rome. This was sent to the King, with the notice of the day that was prefixed for the return of his answer, and with other motives which must have been very great, since they prevailed so much."[2]

---

[1] Burnet, *op. cit.*, Vol. I, p. 213.
[2] *Ibid.*, p. 213.

What happened next ?   Our preceding paragraph refers solely to the Bishop of Paris and to steps taken at Rome as the result of his intervention in Henry's name.   It seems to us that there is a contradiction between what we are about to write and what we have already transcribed about the King's unwillingness to " abase himself so far as to send any submission in writing."   It may be that the apparent inconsistency is due to the fact that Henry, running true to form, changed his mind.   Be this as it may, the text from which we are quoting informs us that : " In answer there was a courier dispatched from the King with a formal promise under his hand."[1]

If Henry agreed in this way " to abase himself so far as to send a submission in writing " why was it that nothing came of his going to Canossa ?   We know that he was " in so good hope of his business that he sent Sir Edward Karne to Rome to prosecute his suit."[2]   Once more let the author of *The History of the Reformation* speak for us.   He proclaims that :

" The courier arrived from England with the King's submission under his hand in due form, and earnest letters from the French King to have it accepted, that so the business might be composed. When this was known at Rome, all the indifferent and wise Cardinals (among whom was Farnese that was afterwards Pope Paul the Third) came to the Pope, and desired that it might be again considered

[1] Burnet, *op. cit.*, Vol. I, p. 214.
[2] *Ibid.*, p. 215.

before it went further. So it was brought again into the Consistory."[1]

The Bible tells of a scapegoat and of Aaron presenting him to the Lord for a sin offering. Burnet, face to face with the dual fact (1) that a " courier arrived from England, with the King's submission under his hand in due form " and (2) that the Pope did not do what Henry wanted, found the necessary scapegoat in those whom he calls " the indifferent and wise Cardinals " and the " Imperialists." It seems that " they so managed the matter, that it was confirmed anew by the Pope and the Consistory, and they ordered the Emperor to execute the sentence."[2]

This decision threw Henry into a rage. When he " heard it and understood that he was used with so much scorn and contempt at Rome, being all the more vexed because he had come to such a submission, he resolved then to break totally from Rome."[3] We can well understand why the King was so much incensed. The letter to him from the Archbishop of York and the Bishop of Duresme, dated May 11th, 1534, of which we have already spoken, makes it clear that he and those in his confidence believed that they had inside information that Clement would decide in their favour. This language arrests our attention :

" The Pope . . . declared unto him . . . that if your Grace would send a Proxie thither, hee

---

[1] Burnet, *op. cit.*, Vol. I, p. 215.
[2] *Ibid.*, p. 215.
[3] *Ibid.*, p. 215.

would give the sentence for your Highness against her, because that he knew that your Cause was good and just, which his saying was according also to an Epistle Decretall sent hither by the Legat Campegius, whereof the effect was, that if Marriage and carnall knowledge were had betwixt Prince Arthur and her, the Legates should pronounce for the Divorce."[1]

John Heywood, who was a contemporary of Henry's children, wrote that :

" Reckeners without their host must recken twice." When a litigant—and the King was a litigant—proceeds on the theory that occult influences permit him to know in advance what a judge's decision is going to be, he should bear this trite saying in mind—and he should recall Henry's experience.

We have no patience with him for having put himself in this ludicrous position. He should have known that, if he and his agents had attempted to corrupt Clement's advisers and if he had spent thousands of ducats in endeavouring to do so, the Pope, at every crucial point in this entire case, had given irrefutable evidence of his incorruptibility and of his fearlessness. " Forewarned is forearmed " runs another old adage. The King's lack of judgment " in coming to such a submission " when he should have known that he could neither buy nor coerce Clement, drives home the point that

[1] Herbert, *op. cit.*, p. 375.

he was a wayward boy who refused to permit experience to make a man of him.

A few months after the King launched the English schism[1] or, as Herbert puts it, after " he separated himself from the Obedience of the Roman Church, but not from the Religeon thereof (some few articles only excepted) as they shall appear hereafter,"[2] the Pope died. The exact date of his death was September 25th, 1534. Parliament and most of the clergy were then in complete subjection to Henry, who exercised both temporal and spiritual authority. Nevertheless the old Faith numbered a majority of adherents in England far into the reign of Elizabeth.[3]

The great Catholic scholar who has written the masterly *History of the Popes* holds Clement responsible because England has strayed away from the Catholic Church. His indictment is drawn in these terms :

" It does not admit of doubt that he (Clement) was wanting in the necessary resolution to intervene firmly and, before it was too late, place an imperative alternative before Henry VIII. As the King had come forward decidedly against Luther, his threats of apostasy had not been taken seriously at Rome where, hoping against hope, it was thought that time would cool the adulterous passion which had reached a pitch of frenzy. The Pope, therefore, adopted a dilatory policy, did not speak out at once . . . and did injury to the interests of the Church."[4]

[1] Pastor, *op. cit.*, Vol. X, p. 287.
[2] Herbert, *op. cit.*, p. 369.
[3] Brewer, *op. cit.*, Vol. II, p. 469.
[4] Pastor, *op. cit.*, Vol. X, p. 332.

We enter a demurrer to this indictment. We are not called upon to go beyond this plea because it is unanswerable. The merits of the charge have already been refuted by the facts which are crowded into our pages.

The Pope was the League of Nations of the sixteenth century. His authority, like that of President Wilson's intellectual offspring, was purely moral. He had no army to give executory force to his decisions. He could resort to the weapon of excommunication, but his anathemas were not put into the form of a barrage of shot and shell and did not assume the shape of a commercial blockade. They were entirely spiritual and their effect was dependent upon the appeal they made to the conscience of the civilized world.

Pastor castigates Clement because he hesitated before excommunicating the " Defender of the Faith." We retort : if the Council of the League of Nations were to be convinced that to-morrow one of its moral edicts was destined to encounter from the civilization of the twentieth century the same reception that Clement's anathema received from that of the sixteenth, would it be tempted to issue it ?

Pastor, in levelling his charges against the Pope, forgot that society was in a fluid state when Clement reigned. The Catholic Church had successfully confronted the rise and fall of the Middle Ages because she was equipped to meet the conditions which they begat. With the dawn of a new era new problems arose.

The advent of this changed mentality called for "printing-press" men to cope with it. It was not until Ignatius of Loyola appeared upon the scene and created the Jesuit order that Catholicism had the intellectual shock troops called for by the emergency. Under the impulse of Jesuit leadership the era of steam, the century of electricity and the decades of the wireless have not only found the Church of Rome stronger than ever but they see her awaiting with confidence and complacency the many other startling inventions that are still in the womb of time.

History has been most unfair to Clement VII. Attacked in Germany by the eloquence of Luther and in England by a King whose superstitions and smattering of theology were used by designing men and an ambitious woman for their own ends, he died in the breach because he had no mobile army to come to his aid. The Italians say that "*il tempo è sempre galant'uomo*"—that time is always a gentleman. These words suggest themselves to our mind when we contemplate the injustice that has been done to his memory.

INDEX

PRINTED IN GREAT BRITAIN BY
MACKAYS LIMITED, CHATHAM